Pension Policy

for a

Mobile Labor Force

John A. Turner
U.S. Department of Labor

with
Tabitha A. Doescher
and
Phyllis A. Fernandez

1993

W.E. UPJOHN INSTITUTE for Employment Research
Kalamazoo, Michigan

HD
7125
·T85
1993

Library of Congress Cataloging-in-Publication Data

Turner, John A.
  Pension policy for a mobile labor force / John A. Turner with
Tabitha Doescher and Phyllis Fernandez.
      p.   cm.
  Includes bibliographical references and index.
  ISBN 0-88099-133-X (pbk.) : ISBN 0-88099-134-8 (cloth)
    1. Pensions—United States.   2. Occupational mobility—United
States.   3. Pension trusts—United States.   4. Retirement income—
United States.   I. Doescher, Tabitha.   II. Fernandez, Phyllis.
III. Title.
HD7125.T85   1993
331.25'2'0973—dc20   92-47019
                                                                         CIP

The facts presented in this study and the observations and viewpoints expressed are the
sole responsibility of the authors. They do not necessarily represent positions of the
W.E. Upjohn Institute for Employment Research.

Cover design by J.R. Underhill.
Index prepared by Shirley Kessel.
Printed in the United States of America.

PREFACE

Concern about retirement income adequacy has caused policymakers to search for ways to reduce pension benefit losses of job changers. This book surveys the pension policy issues relating to job change and analyzes the potential impact of proposed policy changes. Chapter 3 was co-authored and chapter 5 was authored by Phyllis Fernandez. Chapters 6 and 11 were written by Tabitha Doescher. The authors received helpful comments from Alan Gustman, Edwin Hustead, Joanne Brodsky, and two anonymous reviewers. Editorial assistance was provided by Elizabeth Sherman and Judith Gentry.

Material presented in this book does not represent the position of the U.S. Department of Labor or of any other organizations with which the authors are associated.

The Author

John A. Turner is Deputy Director of the Office of Research and Economic analysis, Pension and Welfare Benefits Administration, U.S. Department of Labor. He has written or edited five books on pensions and employer-provided health benefits, one of which has been translated into Japanese. His books include *Trends in Pensions 1992, Trends in Health Benefits,* and *Pension Policy: An International Perspective.* He has written numerous articles on pension and social security policy. He has a Ph.D. in economics from the University of Chicago.

CONTENTS

LIST OF TABLES

1

Job Mobility
and
Pension Portability

Movement and change enliven American culture. Nowhere is that more evident than in the labor market. But employers create a conflict between job mobility and retirement security when they cut future pension benefits for workers who quit a job before reaching retirement age. Presumably, employers do this to discourage workers from changing jobs.

Neither U.S. workers nor employers commit to a lifetime contract. After several early-career job changes, however, workers often do stay permanently with one employer. Once they reach age 40, one of two male and one of four female workers remain on the same job until retirement 20 to 25 years later (Quinn, Burkhauser, and Myers 1990, p. 34). Jobs with pensions promote even more job stability, especially for women.

Job change contributes to an efficient labor market, increasing market flexibility and aiding economic growth and competitiveness. Pensions, conversely, bind workers to jobs, and possibly allocate resources inefficiently. Employers, some argue, should be encouraged to restructure pension plans so that they no longer discourage workers from changing jobs. Need for such restructuring is heightened by the aging of the U.S. workforce, since job mobility declines as workers grow older.

Many employers favor little job change, however, preferring a stable workforce. Longevity is the benefit employers expect in exchange for their investment in worker skills. Workers do leave jobs, however. They quit for personal or family reasons, such as the relocation of a spouse or the need to care for a child or an elderly parent, or they are laid off—frequently for reasons beyond their control.

HISTORY OF U.S. PENSIONS

A brief history of pension coverage in the United States provides background for the discussion of pension portability. Private pension plans began during the last quarter of the nineteenth century.[1] By 1930 many large employers, including AT&T, General Electric, and DuPont, had pension plans. The number of plans stopped growing during the Depression, but resumed growth in the 1940s. From 1940 to 1972 pension coverage of full-time workers rose from 17 to 52 percent.

Pension coverage grew through 1970 due to union collective bargaining in retail, construction, manufacturing, transportation, and mining industries. In industries with many small unionized firms, multiemployer defined benefit plans administered jointly by a union and an employer-appointed board of trustees are the most common plan type. Large unionized firms typically have defined benefit plans, as well.

Since the early 1970s pension coverage has fallen slightly, and basic coverage has shifted from defined benefit toward defined contribution plans. Firms also increasingly have provided defined contribution plans to supplement benefits for workers already covered by a defined benefit plan.

Defined contribution plans covered one-third of the workers in plans started before 1975, but they have covered four-fifths of the workers in plans started after 1975. In 1975, 78 percent of the participants in pension plans were in primary defined benefit plans. By 1989 that number had fallen to 64 percent, and a projection suggests that by 2000 the figure will have fallen to 51 percent (Hay/Huggins 1990a).

Pension coverage changes since the early 1970s have been due largely to changes in the labor force. Coverage remains high among large firms and among unionized firms. Such firms are employing a falling share of the labor force, however, and employment has grown rapidly in small nonunionized firms in service industries. Pension coverage has always been low among workers in these firms.

The fastest growing industries from 1979 to 1988 were services and specifically finance, insurance, and real estate. Pension coverage rates also rose most rapidly in those groups: from 30 to 38 percent for service industry workers, and from 54 to 59 percent for finance, insurance, and real estate workers. Those industry coverage gains offset somewhat a drop in workers employed in manufacturing, where coverage had been high. The large shift in jobs to the service sector, however, with its below-average coverage rate, depressed pension coverage rates.

PRIVATE PENSIONS AND JOB CHANGE

When private pensions were started in the late 1800s, firms used them to charitably retire older workers whose productivity was waning. The plans also helped maintain a loyal workforce. Firms frequently did not provide pensions to "early leavers"—workers leaving before retirement.

Expectations have changed. Workers now commonly view pensions as deferred pay that even short-tenure employees have a right to accrue. These expectations, plus concern about retirement income adequacy, make pension benefit loss incurred by job leavers a public policy issue affecting the majority of the workforce. In 1988, 68 percent of males and 51 percent of females working full time were in a private pension plan in either their current or a past job. Of all full-time workers with over 15 years on their current job, 78 percent had participated in a pension in a current or past job. Twenty-three percent of full-time workers age 45 to 54 had been in a pension plan on a prior job (Piacentini 1990b).

Worker myopia when changing jobs may cause low retirement income. Due to the growth of defined contribution plans, which commonly allow job leavers to cash out, employers frequently pay preretirement lump sums to departing employees. In the late 1980s, 60 percent of vested job leavers received at least partial lump sum cashouts of their pension benefits. Fifty-one percent of vested job leavers received lump sum benefits for their entire pension (Piacentini 1990b).

Because so many job leavers cash out their pensions, some policymakers argue that federal law on pension policy should lock-in pension benefits. When workers and employers do not react to this restriction by reducing the generosity of plans, locking-in pension benefits raises net savings in pensions. Higher savings via pensions not offset by a fall in other savings raise gross individual and national savings.

Because pensions often reward long tenure through various plan features, and because there is little or no portability, job leavers frequently end up with lower benefits than job stayers, even when they do not cash out their pensions. Consider two workers with equal incomes through their careers. Worker A spends his/her career with one employer, while worker B changes employers several times. Worker A will receive a much larger pension than B, even if B's employers had pension plans identical to those of A. The benefits differ solely due to B having changed jobs.

PENSION REFORM FOR A MOBILE LABOR FORCE

Three labor market changes form the background against which pension reform is considered. First, intermittent workers have difficulty accumulating adequate retirement income. With more women entering the workforce, federal retirement income policy is challenged by some women's small retirement incomes due to their discontinuous work histories. Also, workers in some industries have high job turnover, making it less likely that they will accumulate sufficient pension benefits to ensure adequate retirement income.

Second, social security expansion has ended, and a slight contraction is predicted. Social security is projected to pay less generous benefits relative to earnings during the early part of the twenty-first century (Doescher and Turner 1988). This places pressure on private pensions and individual savings to raise retirement income in order to offset the contraction. Third, jobs have shifted to economic sectors having low pension coverage rates and relying less on defined benefit plans. These changes affect the options available to job leavers who are covered by a pension.

Defined Contribution and Defined Benefit Plans

To understand pension policy, one must understand the basic ways defined contribution and defined benefit plans differ. Defined contribution plans allocate employer contributions to individual accounts like savings or mutual funds accounts. Such plans require employers to contribute a fixed share of pay or allow employers to vary contributions (as in a profit-sharing plan). Defined contribution plans may accept worker contributions, and often require them as a condition for matching employer contributions. Assets are typically pooled for investing. Investment gains and losses are allocated *pro rata* to worker accounts, and the worker bears the investment risk. In these plans, a worker's pension benefit at retirement equals the accumulated contributions plus investment earnings and losses allocated to the account. The employer may pay the account balance to the worker as a lump sum, pay it out over a period of time, or use it to purchase an annuity paying benefits for a specified period, like 20 years, or for life.

Defined benefit plans promise a retirement benefit figured by a formula, which usually includes earnings and tenure. The formula, for example, might be $20 a month times years of tenure with the employer, or it might be 1 percent of final salary times tenure. In defined benefit plans, the employer must make contributions—figured by an actuary under government regulation—sufficient to fund the promised benefits. When investment earnings fall short of promised benefits, the employer is financially responsible for the shortfall. Pension beneficiaries may share risk, however, by receiving smaller cost-of-living increases when the firm or the plan does poorly.

Effects of Benefit Loss from Job Change

When job leavers lose pension benefits they also lose tax benefits afforded by pensions. This raises questions about tax equity. Should tax benefits reward job tenure? Because long job tenure has been more common among men than women, does this policy discriminate against women?

Pension benefit loss deters workers from changing jobs or careers. The "golden handcuff" effect may lower economic efficiency by preventing workers from moving to their most productive job situation. This problem may be critical in declining industries that need to shrink but have tied workers to jobs by pensions. Similarly, if pensions have inhibited job change, they have hampered the labor market's ability to adjust.

Rather than worrying about golden handcuffs, however, some analysts are concerned about short job tenure. They argue that Japanese lifetime jobs encourage employers and workers to invest in worker productivity. Long tenure with an employer may be needed to recoup the investment from job-specific training. Thus, while both training and eliminating barriers to worker mobility are critical for fully using U.S. human resources, the goals conflict.

Pension Portability

Pension portability has been defined as the capacity to carry pension benefits from one job to the next. It has been closely linked to preserving vested benefits when a worker ends a job before retirement. The portability concept has recently been expanded to include accrued but unvested benefits. Of more importance, analysts have recognized that even when vested, job leavers' benefits erode in value due to inflation, reducing the real value of vested pension benefits; thus, the portability concept has expanded to mean preserving the real value of pension benefits when a worker ends a job before retirement.[2] Portability loss is the shortfall of actual retirement benefits from benefits that would have been paid had the worker not changed jobs.

Pension portability is achieved in three ways: through portability of benefits, service, or assets. Benefits are portable when the worker has a vested right to accrued benefits. With vesting, a worker changes jobs without losing nominal pension benefits, but the benefits can erode in real value due to inflation. Service is portable when years of service under a prior employer's plan count in figuring pension benefits with a new employer. Service portability is found in multiemployer plans, but also could be achieved by wage or price indexing the benefits of job leavers. These options reduce real benefit loss for workers changing jobs.

Pension assets are portable when the worker receives a cash distribution of accrued benefits and rolls it over to an Individual Retirement Account (IRA) or another employer-provided pension plan. Asset portability is commonly available in defined contribution plans, and is increasingly available in defined benefit plans. Asset portability is often called "preservation" because the rollover or interplan transfer preserves preretirement cashouts as retirement savings.

Corresponding to the three avenues to pension portability, there are three ways a job leaver may lose pension benefits. First, workers lose benefits by not having worked long enough to vest (deferred vesting).

Second, workers lose benefits because plans offer lower benefits for workers who quit before retirement (design aspects of pension plans). This loss includes those cases where employers base cost-of-living adjustments on tenure. Third, workers lose benefits by treating the pension plan as severance pay rather than a retirement plan (consuming benefits before retirement). All three losses may be the result of a voluntary decision to change jobs or may be due to a layoff.

Legislative changes requiring vesting after five years for most workers have reduced portability losses incurred from nonvesting. Approximately one-third of the remaining portability losses are due to other aspects of plan design, while two-thirds are due to workers cashing out benefits before they retire. Options for reducing portability losses due to plan design, on the one hand, and worker behavior, on the other, would distribute benefit costs differently. Plan design options could be expected to raise benefits accrued by short-term workers. Worker behavior options, by contrast, do not affect accrued benefits, but influence what workers do with these benefits.

Other countries have reduced pension portability losses more than the United States. Such policies include shorter vesting (Canada), a government or private clearinghouse for job leaver benefits (Netherlands, Japan), indexed benefits in defined benefit plans for workers quitting prior to retirement (United Kingdom), and a ban on lump sum payments to job leavers (Netherlands, Canada).

In 1972, Dan McGill wrote a book analyzing U.S. pension portability and focusing largely on pension vesting. When McGill wrote, nonvesting caused a major share of portability losses. Since 1972, the U.S. pension system has changed dramatically. The Employee Retirement Income Security Act of 1974 (ERISA) set minimum vesting standards which have since been tightened; now most workers vest within five years in a private pension plan.

Pension analysts have increasingly realized that vested workers lose benefits by changing jobs, however, and that those losses greatly reduce the benefit protection that vesting was thought to provide. Though pension portability has been an issue for many years, the remarkable changes in the U.S. pension system, the changes in the U.S. labor market, and better understanding of pension economics have raised the portability issues this book addresses.

OUTLINE OF THE BOOK

This book analyzes what happens to the pension benefits of workers who quit or are laid off jobs. Presenting empirical evidence wherever possible, the book progresses from an overview to an informal analysis using simple logic and descriptive data, then proceeds to a more formal analysis using economic theory and econometric studies.

The first six chapters of the book describe why pension benefit losses are a significant problem and examines the number of workers affected and the amount of loss they incur. As background on quits and layoffs, chapter 2 portrays a labor market undergoing changes that often result in reductions in retirement benefits. Chapter 3 further describes job change by examining data on individual workers, and the particular impact of mobility on women's pension benefits. Job mobility often reduces future pension benefits, and chapter 4 investigates the size of these losses. Chapter 5 examines receipt and subsequent use of preretirement lump sum distributions, which constitute two-thirds of portability losses. Chapter 6 discusses issues concerning the pension benefits of laid-off workers.

Chapters 7 through 12 analyze possible policy responses to the pension benefit loss of job changers. Chapter 7 describes pension plan features that already reduce portability losses. Chapter 8 debates the pros and cons of pension portability reform in five areas: equity, tax and budget policy, regulation, economic effects, and financial responsibility. Chapter 9 describes and evaluates policy options designed to reduce portability losses. Chapter 10 examines how policies mandating portability would affect employers and workers. It also surveys studies relating pensions and job change, because some portability policies may increase job change. Chapter 11 examines the role of layoffs in portability losses. Chapter 12 discusses policies towards pension portability in Canada, Japan, the Netherlands, and the United Kingdom. These countries have pension systems similar to that of the United States, yet each has dealt differently with portability. Chapter 13 concludes the book with a selective list of policies that would reduce the pension benefit losses of job changers.

Several issues related to pension portability have been omitted from the discussion. The first is greater pension coverage. While it would further a goal of portability—to raise retirement benefits—it is not itself a portability issue. The second is pension loss when a plan ends. Like the loss when a worker separates from an employer, some policies for dealing with those losses—such as indexing benefits—are the same. But as with coverage, considering these issues would greatly expand the book. The third issue is firm-initiated early retirement for older workers. Though not considered here, many pension issues for these older workers are the same as those for younger workers facing a layoff. The fourth omitted issue is pension portability in the public sector. The book deals only with the private sector, although public sector workers face similar pension issues.

NOTES

1. Much of the discussion of pension coverage is based on Beller and Lawrence (1992).

2. Some analysts define portability more narrowly, distinguishing the ability to transfer benefit rights between jobs from the preservation of real vested benefit rights with a former employer.

2

The Changing
U.S. Labor Market

The U.S. labor market changed greatly during the 1980s and early 1990s, causing many workers to switch jobs and affecting the way in which firms provide pensions. These shifts created the context and need for pension portability. This chapter describes economic changes that have caused workers to seek new jobs and explores the magnitude of that mobility. The chapter provides background information on changes in employment by industry and changes in unionization factors that affect the need for pension portability. It also discusses changes in the pension system over the past decade, in particular the trend towards defined contribution plans and away from defined benefit plans.

LABOR MARKET SHIFTS

Shifts in the U.S. economy have affected how workers accumulate benefits for retirement. One of these changes is the shift toward the service sector and away from manufacturing. Three-fourths of new jobs in the 1980s were in services and retail trades.[1] From 1979 to 1988 the percentage of full-time private-sector wage and salary workers employed in services rose from 19 to 24 percent. The percentage employed in finance, insurance, and real estate rose from 7 to 9 percent. By contrast, factory jobs in 1988 fell to 1.7 million below the peak in 1979. From 1972 to 1988 the share of the full-time employed labor force in manufacturing fell from 34 to 28 percent (Beller and Lawrence 1992).

Changes in Employment by Industry

During the 1980s the mining industry suffered an astounding 25 percent job loss, while manufacturing suffered a 7 percent loss. In contrast, government, transportation, and public utilities, the slowest-growing service sector industries, each grew 11 percent.

Job shifts for narrower industrial classifications were even greater. Half of mining jobs are in oil and gas extraction, which grew by 50 percent during the decade's first three years as the price of crude petroleum soared. The number of wells drilled and oil rigs erected, as well as the price of crude oil all peaked in 1982 and then plummeted to less then half the peak by 1987. Jobs in oil and gas extraction followed the same pattern, hitting an all-time high in 1982 and then falling: all jobs gained earlier in the decade, plus 75,000 more, were lost by 1987. Coal mining suffered even more than oil and gas during the 1980s, with job loss reaching 46 percent. Copper and iron mining jobs fell 60 percent over the decade.

In contrast, construction employment grew during the 1980s. Being sensitive to business cycles, the industry lost jobs during the two recessions early in the decade, but expanded rapidly over the next three years with the onset of economic recovery and a sharp drop in interest rates. Growth continued throughout the rest of the decade, with jobs in the special trades category—carpentry, masonry, electrical work, and roofing—growing by 850,000.

The long 1980s expansion triggered growth in other areas. Changing lifestyles, such as women working more outside the home, contributed to retail trade growth. More spending power and less free time affected services trades, with eating and drinking establishments heading the industries adding the most jobs in the 1980s: one of every 10 jobs added over the decade. One of every 20 jobs gained over the decade was in a grocery store.

Gross Employment Flows

These employment changes, dramatic though they are, understate total job changes. These shifts in industry employment are net changes—the net workers leaving or entering.[2]

Since in most industries workers are continuously entering and leaving, net employment changes are smaller than gross changes. Within industries some firms grow while others decline. Within firms, workers are fired or quit in some departments while workers are hired in others. Several studies find large gross employment flows caused by firms opening, growing, shrinking, and closing (Leonard 1987; Dunne, Roberts, and Samuelson 1989).

During the early 1980s, one in eight jobs every year was new, while one in nine jobs was destroyed. Job creation is defined as the share of net jobs added at growing firms, while job destruction signifies jobs lost at shrinking firms (Leonard 1987). In an average quarter during the early 1980s, 6 percent of manufacturing jobs disappeared and 5 percent were created (Davis and Haltiwanger 1989).

EMPLOYER-PROVIDED PENSIONS

These labor market changes have affected a number of pension variables: which employers provide pensions; which workers are covered; and what plans are used. The changes also have affected the amount of pension benefits lost with job change and the types of policy changes that would prevent these losses from occurring.

Changes in worker coverage rates by industry from 1972 to 1988 varied by gender, union status, and firm size. Within each industry the coverage rate for women gained relative to men—the coverage rate among women workers rose from 25 to 35 percent in services, and from 46 to 60 percent in the finance, insurance, and real estate sector. For females, who are disproportionately in the service industry and the finance, insurance, and real estate sector, the coverage rate rise in these industries contributed to the rise in rate of overall female coverage. The rise in percentage of males working in low-coverage service industry jobs resulted in the fall of male coverage rate.

While the pension coverage rate for nonunionized workers rose from 40 to 44 percent from 1979 to 1988, the rate for full-time workers in a collective bargaining unit remained at 78 percent. Coverage among nonunionized workers rose in all major industry divisions except for transportation, communications, and utilities. This increase, however, offset the loss of high-coverage union jobs. The percentage of the labor force that was unionized fell from 27 to 17 percent between 1979 and 1988. The decline in union coverage took place in all major industries, with the greatest drop occurring in services.

Pension plan coverage also closely correlates with firm size. In 1988, coverage rates ranged from 16 percent for workers in firms employing fewer than 25 workers to 73 percent for firms with 1,000 or more employees. Workers reporting employment in firms with 1,000 or more employees fell from 41 to 39 percent of the labor force from 1979 to 1988.

Type of Plan

While the primary pension plan for most workers is a defined benefit plan, defined contribution plans are becoming increasingly popular. In the late 1980s, primary defined benefit plans covered one-third of workers, while primary defined contribution plans covered one-sixth (Turner and Beller 1992); however, 73 percent of primary defined benefit plans were offered in combination with secondary defined contribution plans by 1984 (Bodie and Papke 1990).

Defined benefit plans, which are found predominantly in union firms, large firms, and manufacturing firms (Kotlikoff and Smith 1983), have fallen in importance as a source of pension coverage. After reaching a peak coverage rate of 40 percent of private full-time workers in the early 1970s, defined benefit coverage declined to 31 percent in 1987. Between 1980 and 1989 this coverage dropped from 30.1 million to 27.2 million workers, and the decline has continued into the early 1990s.

In contrast, defined contribution plan popularity has risen in recent years, due in large part to the popularity of 401(k) plans. In 1975, only 15 percent of full-time workers participated in defined contribution plans. By 1987, 30 percent were covered by a defined contribution plan. The Revenue Act of 1978 added Section 401(k) to the IRS Tax Code, effective for taxable years beginning after December 31, 1979. Under a 401(k) plan, workers choose between cash or contributions to a trust. The latter are made before taxes. Data for 1988 show 12.3 million workers, or 17 percent of full-time private wage and salary workers, were in a 401(k) plan. The 401(k) plans covered 18 percent of full-time male workers and 15 percent of full-time female workers. One policy concern is that the shift toward defined contribution plans, boosted by 401(k) plans, could lead to lower future pension benefits because job leavers often cash out those plans.

Several reasons have been advanced for the shift from defined benefit to defined contribution coverage, including employment shifts from industries with large and unionized firms, but also legislation—which imposed costly compliance for defined benefit plans but improved tax treatment for some defined contribution plans. Firms with a defined benefit plan have, on average, cut 3 percent of covered workers between 1975 and 1987. They cut more than 10 percent in mining, construction, manufacturing, transportation, and wholesale trade. Coverage under the defined benefit plans of the big three U.S. automakers alone fell 22 percent from 1975 to 1987 (a 210,000 worker loss).

Dual Coverage

Many workers are covered both by a defined benefit plan and a supplemental defined contribution plan. Supplemental coverage of workers by a second plan is highest in industries with a high coverage rate under primary plans. Manufacturing industry workers have a 65 percent coverage rate. Of those covered, 50 percent are also enrolled in a supplemental plan. Only mining has a high coverage rate (64 percent) combined with a below average supplemental coverage rate (37 percent). Supplemental defined contribution plans enable employers to offer extra benefits at reduced cost; 56 percent of these plans are funded to some extent by worker contributions.

Concluding Comments

Major economic changes have significantly affected the way in which firms provide pensions. This chapter has examined job changes and the characteristics of employers providing and workers covered by pensions from an aggregate perspective. The next chapter examines these issues from the perspective of individual workers, focusing on the attributes of employees changing jobs. Taken together, these two chapters describe changes in the U.S. labor market and provide the background for understanding the pension issues arising from these changes.

NOTES

1. This discussion is drawn from Plunkert (1990).

2. Net changes are the difference between total workers entering an industry and total workers leaving the industry. Gross changes are the total workers entering and leaving

3

Characteristics of Job Changers

Because portability issues directly concern job changers, it is important to examine the characteristics of workers who change jobs and to understand the dynamics of job mobility. Is job change increasing over time? How does it vary across age groups and by gender?[1] If the rate of job change were to decrease, would we still need to formulate pension policies to reduce benefit losses incurred by job changers? How do portability policies affect men and women differently? This overview discusses these and related questions by looking at job tenure studies, with particular attention to the impact of portability policies on women.

JOB TENURE IN THE UNITED STATES

Job change can be studied by examining actual tenure and estimating eventual tenure for jobs in progress. Hall (1982) documented the prevalence of lengthy completed job tenure for males and concluded the following:

1. The typical worker holds a job that will last about eight years. Over one-quarter of all workers are employed in jobs that will continue 20 years or more; 60 percent hold jobs that will last five years or more.

2. The jobs held by middle-aged workers with more than 10 years of tenure are extremely stable. Over a decade, only 20 to 30 percent of these workers move.

3. Among workers aged 30 and older, 40 percent are currently working in jobs at which they will remain for 20 or more years. Three-quarters are in jobs at which they will remain for five or more years.

4. The duration of employment among blacks is as long as that among whites. Even though jobs held by blacks are worse along almost every other dimension, they are no less stable than those held by whites.

5. Women remain on jobs a substantially shorter period of time than men. Only one-quarter of women over age 30 are employed in jobs they will occupy for more than 20 years, whereas over one-half of men over age 30 hold these near-lifetime jobs.

While Hall found that by age 44 workers had held an average of 8.5 jobs, he also found that one-half of those age 40 to 44 who have been in their current jobs for 5 to 10 years will retain these jobs an additional 10 years. Job changes generally occur in the first few years after employment begins. Young workers change jobs a great deal until they find a good career match.

Sehgal (1984) states that employment data from the January 1983 CPS support the contention that mature American workers, on average, show substantial job stability. The survey asked whether participants were engaged in the kind of work they had been doing a year earlier, how long they had done that kind of work, and how long they had been working continuously for their current employer. Sehgal's principal findings on tenure are the following:

1. One worker in six has been with his/her employer for at least 15 years.

2. Among workers age 45 and over, nearly one-third have been with their current employer for 20 years or more.

3. Tenure with one's employer is closely linked to tenure in one's occupation.

Looking at gender differences in tenure, Sehgal's findings show that one male worker in five has been with his employer for at least 15 years, while one female worker in 10 has been with her employer for that period. Among workers age 45 and over, 38 percent of men and 16 percent of women have been with their current employer 20 years or more.

Mitchell (1986) discusses job attachment among older workers while focusing on gender differences in job tenure. She also uses data from the January 1983 Current Population Survey and a methodology similar to that of Hall (1982). Table 3.1 presents differences in tenure by sex. It shows the greatest contrast among men and women workers to be found in the longer-tenure groups. Only 4 percent of working women have been on their jobs for 20 or more years, compared to 12 percent of men. In addition, 38.8 percent of all males but only 13.3 percent of all females are likely to complete 20 or more years. This supports Hall's 1978 data, which show these figures as 37.3 percent and 15.1 percent. At the other extreme, the table shows 54 percent of males and 67 percent of females spending fewer than five years with their current employers.

Table 3.1
Tenure to Date and Eventual Tenure by Sex, 1983

Tenure (years)	Males (percent)		Females (percent)		F/M	
	Actual	Eventual)	Actual	Eventual	Actual	Eventual
Less than 1	24.5	14.2	30.3	17.9	1.2	1.3
1-4	29.9	22.3	36.6	31.7	1.2	1.4
5-9	16.6	10.6	16.3	16.0	1.0	1.5
10-14	19.2	7.5	8.4	11.7	0.4	1.6
15-19	7.0	7.6	4.3	9.8	0.6	1.3
20 or more	11.9	38.8	4.2	13.3	0.4	0.3

SOURCE: January 1983 Current Population Survey data as compiled in Mitchell (1986).
NOTE: All figures are adjusted by sex-specific survival rates as in Horvath (1983). The survival rate is the ratio of 1x values from a standard life table. These values represent the number of persons of 100,000 born alive still living at the beginning of the age interval.

Table 3.2 presents eventual tenure of prime age and older workers and shows clearly that tenure is shorter for women than men across all age groups. Women aged 40 and over are only half as likely as men to complete 20 or more years of tenure—23.3 percent versus 56.4 percent.

These tables suggest the following conclusions:

1. The majority of jobs last fewer than five years for both sexes; relatively short-term employment is not confined to women.

2. The most striking gender differences in actual tenure patterns are concentrated not in the short-tenure groups, (e.g. fewer than five years), but rather in the longer-tenure groups. Using eventual tenure data, sex differences become more pronounced between five and ten years, and grow larger thereafter. This means that sex differences in tenure are not primarily due to more "churning" among females starting new jobs.

20

Table 3.2
Distribution of Eventual Tenure by Sex for Prime Age and Older Workers

Eventual years of tenure	Percent age 40-49			Percent age 50-59			Percent age 60+		
	Male	Female	F/M	Male	Female	F/M	Male	Female	F/M
0-4	15.3	26.8	1.8	14.4	20.3	1.4	15.3	20.6	1.3
5-9	9.3	16.2	1.7	10.6	18.0	1.7	16.2	20.3	1.3
10-14	9.7	18.9	1.9	10.9	22.3	2.1	11.1	17.6	1.6
15-19	10.0	15.7	1.6	8.2	14.3	1.7	6.3	10.2	1.6
20 or more	56.4	23.3	0.4	56.5	26.7	0.5	51.0	31.3	0.6

SOURCE: January 1983 Current Population Survey data as compiled in Mitchell (1986).

3. Older women are proportionately more likely to have five or more years of eventual tenure (on their current job) than are their younger counterparts, while the male ratios remain relatively constant across age groups. Therefore, the sex differential in medium- and long-term eventual tenure shrinks with age. However, women age 40 and over are still only half as likely to complete 20 or more years of tenure as men. If women workers in the 1990s follow the same tenure patterns as their predecessors, the labor market will experience reduced average tenure and greater job change in response to the influx of women into the workforce during the last 20 years.

FREQUENCY OF JOB CHANGE

Studies already discussed have alluded to the increasing number of women in the labor force and their effect on job change and labor turnover. To put this in perspective, their share of the total labor force has increased from 32 percent to 46 percent over the 1955-1990 period (*Economic Report of the President 1992*, p. 338).

Table 3.3 indicates that men and women of all age categories have displayed a relatively constant job tenure during the 26-year period from 1951 to 1987, even though the common perception is that people now change jobs more frequently. Women do have lower job tenure than men, however, and the greater proportion of the labor force that is female has increased turnover in the labor force.

Korczyk's (1990) analysis of portability issues for women, however, challenges the standard view of female workers as less attached to the labor force than men. Her review of the literature on portability discusses a study by Haber, Lamas, and Green (1983), which indicates that in 1977 the separation rate for women would have been 1.9 percentage points less than the rate for men if women working full time had been distributed among wage groups in the same way as men. In her own analysis, Korczyk finds that women workers display more job and labor force mobility than men. After controlling for economic and

Table 3.3
Median Years with Current Employer, by Age, Sex, and Race, Selected Years 1951-1987

Worker characteristics	1951	1963	1966	1968	1973	1978	1981	1983	1987
				Years with employer					
Aged 16 years and over[a]									
Men	3.9	5.7	5.2	4.8	4.6	4.5	4.0	5.1	5.0
Women	2.2	3.0	2.8	2.4	2.8	2.6	2.5	3.7	3.6
Difference	1.7	2.7	2.4	2.4	1.8	1.9	1.5	1.4	1.4
25-34 years									
Men	2.8	3.5	3.2	2.8	3.2	2.7	2.9	3.8	3.7
Women	1.8	2.0	1.9	1.6	2.2	1.6	2.0	3.2	3.1
Difference	1.0	1.5	1.3	1.2	1.0	1.1	0.9	0.6	0.6
35-44 years									
Men	4.5	7.6	7.8	6.9	6.7	6.9	6.6	7.7	7.6
Women	3.1	3.6	3.5	2.9	3.6	3.6	3.5	4.6	4.9
Difference	1.4	4.0	4.3	4.0	3.1	3.3	3.1	3.1	2.7
45-54 years									
Men	7.6	11.4	11.5	11.3	11.5	11.0	11.0	13.2	12.3
Women	4.0	6.1	5.7	5.1	5.9	5.9	5.9	6.9	7.3
Difference	3.6	5.3	5.8	6.2	5.6	5.1	5.1	6.3	5.0

White, 16 years and over [a]

Men	4.0	5.9	5.5	5.0	4.7	4.6	4.0	5.3	5.2
Women	2.3	3.0	2.8	2.4	2.8	2.6	2.4	3.6	3.5
Difference	1.7	2.9	2.7	2.6	1.9	2.0	1.6	1.7	1.7

Black, 16 years and over [a,b]

Men	3.1	4.1	3.4	3.3	4.0	3.7	4.0	4.7	4.4
Women	1.7	2.9	2.8	2.0	3.3	3.6	3.3	4.4	4.3
Difference	1.4	1.2	0.6	1.3	0.7	0.1	0.7	0.3	0.1

SOURCE: Compiled by Andrews (1989) from U.S. Department of Commerce, Bureau of the Census, Current Population Reports, Labor Force Series P-50, no. 36 (5 December 1951); Special Labor Force Reports, Bureau of Labor Statistics series on job tenure, nos. 36, 77, 172, and 235; and Bulletin 2162 as quoted for years 1951-1981 by June O'Neill, *Journal of Labor Economics* (January 1985); 1983 data from Ellen Sehgal, "Occupational Mobility and Job Tenure in 1983," *Monthly Labor Review* (October 1984).

a. Age 14 years and over in 1951, 1963, and 1966.
b. Includes other nonwhite races through 1968.

job characteristics, however, these mobility differences narrow, and even change direction.

JOB CHANGE, PORTABILITY, AND WOMEN

Women's mobility makes them more vulnerable to portability loss than men.[2] As their participation in the workforce increases, their need for pension portability grows. The labor force participation rate of women age 20 and older grew from 34 to 58 percent from 1955-91, while that for men declined from 88 to 78 percent (*Economic Report of the President* 1992, p. 338). These figures show women's labor force participation rate relative to men's rose from 38 to 74 percent.

As women's labor force participation has risen and they work more years, their pension coverage rates have also risen. The coverage gap by gender has closed more rapidly than the earnings gap. From 1972 to 1988, women's pension coverage rate rose from 70 to 88 percent of men's. For that period, median weekly earnings of full-time women workers grew from 62 to 72 percent of men's.

Women retiring with pension coverage have lower tenure than men, thus reducing their pension replacement rates because pensions reward long tenure. Data for workers retiring in 1977 and 1978 show a median tenure for female pension beneficiaries of 20 years, compared to 26 for men. Women had a median replacement rate of 18 percent, compared to 22 percent for men (McCarthy 1985).[3] More recent data on replacement rates show that this gap has increased. In 1989, the figures were 17 percent for women and 26 percent for men (Beller and McCarthy 1992).

Women's share of employment differs widely from men's by industry (table 3.4). Women represent more than 40 percent of workers in finance, retail trade, and services, but are represented at a lower rate in other industries. Two-thirds of working women are employed in finance, retail trade, and services, while two-thirds of men are employed in the remaining industries. Because of gender segregation in the labor force, finance, retail trade, and services are referred to as female-dominated industries, while the remaining industries in table 3.4 are referred to as male-dominated.

Table 3.4
Employment and Pension Coverage Rates
by Industry and Gender, 1988

Industry[a]	Percent male	Pension coverage rates (percent)	
		Women	Men
Agriculture	80	15	13
Manufacturing			
Durable goods	74	64	68
Nondurable goods	61	50	66
Trade			
Wholesale	74	38	52
Retail	54	28	31
Services			
Professional	35	43	55
Business and personal	54	19	30
Transportation and public utilities	73	65	60
Construction	92	25	32
Finance, insurance, and real estate	37	59	59
Mining	86	72	62

SOURCE; Korczyk (1992, tables 6.7 and 6.8).
a. Includes self-employed.

The gender mix of an industry's workers dramatically affects pension coverage rates for both sexes. The male pension coverage advantage—6 percentage points for all private sector wage and salary workers—narrows to 2 percentage points in male-dominated industries and disappears in female-dominated industries. For men, working in a male-dominated industry raises the probability of pension coverage from 38 to 55 percent, while working in a male-dominated industry raises the probability for women from 38 to 53 percent.

Vesting and Service Portability

Though women change jobs more frequently than men, vesting rates among women are close to men's. In 1988, 75 percent of women and

80 percent of men in a pension plan had vested benefit rights in their current plan (table 3.5). For workers with a pension on a prior job, 72 percent of women and 70 percent of men were vested in that pension.

Table 3.5
Pension Coverage and Vesting Among Full-Time
Private Sector Workers, by Gender, 1988

	Women		Men	
Employee group[a]	Number (millions)	Percent	Number (millions)	Percent
Total	29.0	100	43.5	100
Pension participants in current or prior job	14.9	51	29.7	68
Current job	12.6	43	21.9	50
Vested	9.5	33	17.4	40
Prior job	4.3	15	8.7	20
Vested	3.1	11	6.2	14
Received lump sum	2.3	8	3.3	8
Current and prior job	2.0	7	4.9	11
No participants in any job	14.1	49	13.8	32

SOURCE: Korczyk (1992, table 6.1).
a. Includes self-employed workers.

Policymakers seeking to reduce pension losses through portability of service presume that a worker leaving a pension-covered job goes to a job with similar coverage. That pattern of job change is less likely to occur for women. The gender distribution among industries suggests that options for continuing pension coverage on later jobs favor men. Women with pensions concentrate in female-dominated industries, where coverage is less common than in male-dominated industries.

If skills, contacts, and other job-related resources are industry-specific, women with pension coverage who change jobs will be less able than men to use employer-oriented portability options because they will be less likely to find another pension-covered job. Portability policies that rely on employers for benefit continuity thus would be less effective for women than policies operating independently of the new employer having a plan—such as indexing vested benefits of job leavers.

Over 70 percent of male pension participants work in male-dominated industries. Nearly 60 percent of female pension participants work in female-dominated industries. Men working full time in male-dominated industries have a coverage rate of 55 percent, versus 38 percent for women working full time in female-dominated industries. Under similar circumstances, therefore, a male pension participant in a male-dominated industry changing jobs within his industry has a 45 percent greater chance of finding a new job with coverage than a female participant in a female-dominated industry [45 = (55 percent/38 percent) -1]. Considering all male and female pension-covered workers, if (1) they change jobs within their industry, and (2) they have a chance equal to the coverage rate for their industry and gender of getting another pension-covered job, 50 percent of males will find coverage compared to 44 percent of females. These figures give males a 6 percentage point, or 14 percent, advantage in odds of finding another job with a pension.

Survey data support the hypothesis that women leaving a pension-covered job are less likely than men to find another pension-covered job. The 1988 Current Population Survey data show 47 percent of female workers with pension coverage on a former job were working on a pension-covered job as of the survey, versus 55 percent of males. Thus, the advantage to males of finding a pension-covered job after leaving one is 17 percent [17 = (55 percent/47 percent) -1], close to the figure estimated above using coverage rates in different industries.

Men with pension coverage are less mobile among jobs than those without coverage, but there is evidence that women's quits are unaffected by pension coverage. Mitchell (1982), using data from the Quality of Employment Survey collected during the 1970s, found men's quit rates were reduced by pension coverage, but women's were not. She conjectures that the women's results may reflect the lower value of pensions for many covered women who only worked intermittently and counted more on spouse retirement benefits than on their own. It could also be explained by women at that time being more likely to work in small firms. Thus, women's greater mobility makes them more vulnerable to portability loss than men.

Preretirement Distributions

Women who have participated in pension plans on prior jobs are far more likely to have received preretirement lump sum distributions than men. For women, 53 percent received a lump sum when they left a pension-covered job, versus 38 percent of men (Korczyk 1992). Thus, portability policy banning lump sum distributions would affect women more. Consistent with their lower earnings, women's preretirement benefit distributions are also much smaller. Although traditionally small distributions are rolled over less frequently than larger distributions, women invest their smaller lump sums and make more use of tax-deferred rollovers. Nearly $3 out of every $10 received by women is rolled over into an IRA or qualified plan, compared to $2 of every $10 received by men.

JOB TENURE AND PENSIONS

Table 3.6 shows job tenure in the context of pension coverage status. This table suggests that pensions are used as a personnel tool to keep workers on the job. The workers covered and participating in a pension in 1988 averaged 10 years of job tenure, while those without coverage averaged 5 years.

Piacentini (1990b) also examined job tenure in relation to pension coverage status. He finds that among full-time private-sector wage and salary workers, one-fourth of pension participants reported current job tenure of 15 or more years, while only 7 percent reported similar tenure when the employer did not sponsor a plan. Twice as many workers with at least 15 years of tenure were in defined benefit plans than defined contribution plans (31 percent versus 16 percent).

In another study, which also examines job tenure as related to pension coverage, Korczyk (1990) found that pension coverage rises significantly with job tenure (table 3.7). With less than one year on the job, fewer than one in eight women are covered by a pension plan, compared to one in six men. In the 1-to-4 years category, the coverage rate rises to just over one in three employees.

Table 3.6
Percentage Distribution of Workers by Tenure at Current Job, 1988

Worker characteristics	Total (000s)	Less than 1	1-4	5-9	10-14	15 or more	Not reported	Mean tenure[a] (years)
				Years of tenure at current job				
Total	72,491	18	34	18	11	15	4	7
Sex								
Male	43,491	17	33	17	11	18	4	8
Female	29,000	19	37	18	10	11	4	6
Race								
White	63,403	18	34	17	11	16	4	7
Black	7,011	18	34	17	12	15	5	7
Other	2,078	18	39	19	10	8	6	5
Age								
16-20	3,429	49	39	2	b	b	10	1
21-24	7,837	33	51	8	c	b	8	2
25-34	24,476	19	43	23	10	2	4	4
35-44	17,788	13	29	20	17	19	3	8
45-54	11,476	9	23	16	13	36	3	12
55-59	4,040	10	18	13	11	44	4	14
60-64	2,385	6	17	17	11	45	3	16
65 or over	1,060	8	16	14	14	44	4	16

Table 3.6 (continued)
Percentage Distribution of Workers by Tenure at Current Job, 1988

Worker characteristics	Total (000s)	Years of tenure at current job						Mean tenure[a] (years)
		Less than 1	1-4	5-9	10-14	15 or more	Not reported	
1988 earnings								
$1-$4,999	2,168	53	24	8	3	5	8	3
$5,000-$9,999	8,085	32	41	10	4	6	7	4
$10,000-$14,999	13,542	22	43	15	7	8	5	5
$15,000-$19,999	11,388	16	39	19	12	12	2	6
$20,000-$24,999	9,648	13	33	20	14	17	3	8
$25,000-$29,999	6,742	10	27	21	16	23	3	9
$30,000-$49,999	11,369	9	28	21	14	26	2	10
$50,000 or more	3,465	7	25	20	17	29	2	11
Not reported	6,085	18	28	16	11	15	11	8
Union status[d]								
Union	10,283	8	22	17	17	34	2	12
Nonunion	56,810	20	37	18	10	12	4	6
Firm size								
Fewer than 10	10,344	22	38	16	8	10	5	6
10-24	6,440	20	42	15	8	10	4	6

25-49	5,462	19	41	18	9	10	4	6
50-99	4,342	22	36	17	8	12	3	6
100-249	5,637	19	38	18	9	12	4	6
250 or more	34,248	13	30	19	13	21	4	9
Not reported	6,019	29	34	13	8	9	7	5
May 1988 pension status[e]							
Noncovered	26,842	26	41	14	7	7	5	5
Coverage unknown	4,575	74	5	1	b	1	20	1
Covered	44,566	13	31	20	13	20	3	9
Nonparticipant	4,782	b	75	15	5	5	c	4
Participation unknown	1,802	26	42	14	6	7	5	5
Participant	34,490	6	27	23	16	25	2	10
Defined benefit[f]	20,484	5	23	22	18	31	2	11
Defined contribution[f]	6,756	6	36	25	15	16	1	8
Plan type not reported	7,250	10	33	22	13	18	4	8

SOURCE: Data from Piacentini (1990b).
a Mean tenure calculations exclude workers not reporting tenure. Workers reporting "less than one year" of tenure are arbitrarily assumed to have one-half year of tenure.
b. No observations in category.
c. Less than 0.5 percent.

Table 3.6 (continued)

d. Workers are classified as union if they reported union membership or coverage under a union contract.

e. A worker is considered to be covered if his or her employer sponsors a pension, retirement, profit sharing, stock, or 401(k)-type plan for any employees, or if he or she reported a secondary self-employed job and contributions to an IRA or Keogh. A worker is considered to be a current pension participant if he or she reported inclusion in a pension, retirement, profit sharing, stock, or 401(k)-type plan at a wage and salary job, or if he or she reported a secondary self-employed job and contribution to an IRA or Keogh.

f. A large degree of response error may be present in worker responses on plan type.

Table 3.7
Job Tenure and Pension Coverage by Gender, 1988

Years with primary employer	All employees[a] (%)	
	Women	Men
Less than 1	20.4	17.3
1-4	38.7	34.1
5-9	18.5	18.1
10-14	10.6	11.7
15-19	6.1	7.0
20 or more	5.7	11.9
All	100.0	100.0
	With pension coverage (%)	
Less than 1	13.4	18.3
1-4	36.6	38.7
5-9	62.5	62.4
1 -14	69.9	72.6
15-19	71.9	77.5
20 or more	75.3	82.2
All	44.6	51.3

SOURCE: Korczyk (1990).
a. Includes self-employed.

MOBILITY AND PENSIONS

A study by Alan Gustman and Thomas Steinmeier (1990) looks at the extent to which workers with current pensions are also likely to be covered on successive jobs. Their findings indicate that one-half to two-thirds of male job changers age 31 to 50 and initially covered by a pension, moved to a job that did not provide coverage. This pattern is found in both the Survey of Consumer Finances (SCF) and in the Survey of Income and Program Participation (SIPP).

Finally, the U.S. Department of Labor has derived the following statistics from the Form 5500 for 1987 on the extent to which workers are
protected against pension benefit loss when they change jobs.[4]

• Fourteen percent of covered workers are in multiemployer plans
  and thus suffer no pension benefit loss for a job change to another
  firm covered by their multiemployer plan.

• An additional 29 percent of covered workers have a defined contribution plan as their primary plan and thus suffer no pension benefit
  loss on that plan when they change jobs and are vested.

• An additional 25 percent of covered workers are covered by a secondary defined contribution plan and suffer no pension benefit loss
  on that plan when they change jobs.

• An additional 4 percent of covered workers are in a defined benefit
  plan that provides preservation of benefits when changing to
  another employer within a portability network, such as the Bell
  Telephone plans.

To summarize these findings, 72 percent of covered workers have
some provision for portability or for preservation of benefits with job
change. Even with this degree of portability and benefit preservation,
an estimated $7 billion in present value of accrued benefits (excluding
lump sum cashouts) was lost due to job changes in 1986.[5]

NOTES

1. This chapter was written by Phyllis Fernandez and John Turner.

2. This discussion is largely based on Korczyk 1990.

3. This replacement rate is calculated as annual pension benefits divided by the average of the
high consecutive three years of earnings.

4. The Form 5500 series report is filed with the Internal Revenue Service annually by each
pension plan in order to disclose information needed to monitor compliance with Employee
Retirement Income Security Act (ERISA) standards.

5. Compiled from the Form 5500 for 1987 by Daniel J. Beller of the Office of Research and
Economic Analysis, Pension and Welfare Benefits Administration, U.S. Department of Labor.

4

Retirement Benefit Loss

When workers change jobs, they often lose retirement benefits. This chapter discusses various pension plan features that cause job leavers to lose pension benefits and the amount of money lost as a result.

MEASURING PORTABILITY LOSS

To clarify alternative measures of portability loss, consider this example. Assume that a worker is in a defined benefit plan, where benefits are based on final pay and years of work. Based on current pay and years of work to date, the worker has accrued a present value of pension benefits of $100. Because retirement is 15 years off and the worker's annual pay increase is about 5 percent, the worker expects final pay to be twice as high as current pay. Based on expected final pay and current years of work, he/she has accrued $200.[1] The $100 is the amount the employee has accrued to date if he/she leaves today. The $200 is the amount the employee has accrued to date if he/she stays until retirement.

Portability loss can be measured three ways: lost net pension wealth; lost gross pension wealth; and lost retirement benefits. The value of net pension wealth depends on whether a "free lunch" exists. The economic argument of no free lunch implies that a worker must exchange higher wages for pension benefits, a tradeoff known as the theory of equalizing differentials.

When a job leaver has given up wages equal to a pension's present value at job change ($100), he/she has no net pension wealth and thus the portability loss is zero. The worker only loses wealth if he/she has overpaid in foregone wages for the retained benefit. If he/she has sacrificed $200 of wages in expectation of a pension based on pay at retirement, the worker suffers a portability loss of $100 by leaving.

The second portability loss metric is lost gross pension wealth in comparison to no job change. Gross pension wealth based on no job change is the present value of accrued *expected* pension benefits based on expected pay at retirement and current tenure. This measure does not net out the wages the worker has foregone to earn the pension benefit. The loss is measured as lost accrued pension benefits, regardless of whether the worker had actually expected to receive those benefits and had paid for them through foregone wages. The worker's gross pension wealth is $200 based on no job change. However, if the worker changes jobs, his/her gross pension wealth is $100. Thus, the portability loss is $100.

A preretirement cashout of benefits is included in net and gross pension wealth because it is a pension payment received by the worker. The worker receives $100 in the cashout, but this is not considered a portability loss because it is not a financial loss to the worker. The receipt of a preretirement cashout thus does not affect portability loss as calculated by the first two measures.

The third metric is the loss of future retirement benefits. Policymakers use this measure most commonly because it stresses the importance of retirement income. By this metric, if a worker changes jobs, he/she loses $100 in future pension benefits—a portability loss. If he/she takes a preretirement cashout and does not reinvest it, he/she suffers a further portability loss of $100 because future retirement benefits are reduced. If the worker changes jobs, cashes out a pension, and does not put the money in another vehicle for retirement savings, he/she has a portability loss of $200. If, however, the cashout is rolled over for retirement savings, it is not considered a portability loss.

Under this metric, job leavers with defined benefit plans lose benefits by changing jobs even if they do not cash out because such plans are based, explicitly or implicitly, on final salary and favor long tenure.[2] Though it may be argued that the short-tenure worker has not yet accrued the benefits awarded to long-tenure workers (because those benefits are based on future salary not yet earned), the worker would have accrued those benefits based on tenure to date had he/she stayed until retirement: the lost benefits are a clear cost of job change.

Some analysts, accepting the first or second measure, argue that if a worker chooses to cash out there is no financial loss. Other analysts argue that a preretirement cash distribution from a pension plan would not be a portability loss if the worker saved it for retirement. Money used to pay down the mortgage, they argue, does not constitute a portability loss because the worker saves the money, albeit in an illiquid form, for retirement. For laid-off unemployed workers, using a cashout to pay the mortgage may be a necessity.

Yet others contend that a worker consuming a cashout could reflect the fact that a given plan had forced the worker to save too much. Cashing out allowed the worker to bring his/her retirement savings in line with expected retirement needs.

A worker losing benefits from one plan may not have reduced his/her retirement income by moving to another, since the pension from the succeeding employer may offset the loss. The worker could further offset a pension loss by raising his/her personal savings, perhaps aided by higher income from the new job.

Thus, while portability losses are commonly considered as losses in a worker's retirement income from a pension, they are not necessarily forfeitures in real wealth because the worker may not yet have paid for those future benefits through lower wages, or may have taken the benefits as a preretirement lump sum payment. Neither is a portability loss necessarily a loss in total retirement income when a worker offsets the portability loss through higher pension benefits on a future job.

WHO SUFFERS PORTABILITY LOSSES?

Workers covered by a pension on a prior job often have suffered a portability loss by changing jobs. Of the full-time 1988 workforce, 18 percent had been covered by a pension on a prior job (table 4.1). Workers who are more likely to be covered by a pension on their current jobs are those who would have been more commonly covered by a pension on a prior job. A higher percentage of male than female full-time workers were covered on a prior job (20 versus 15 percent). The share of workers covered by a pension on a prior job is higher at older ages and higher incomes: of those age 45 to 54, 23 percent were previously covered; of those earning more than $50,000, 33 percent were previously covered. The odds of having lost benefits due to a job change also vary by occupation. Twenty-five percent of managers versus 11 percent of service workers were previously covered.

An indicator of economic loss by workers with pension coverage on a prior job is their current coverage status. Of all workers reporting a pension on a prior job, 69 percent reported having a pension on the current job (table 4.2). The figure is similar for males and females, at 70 and 67 percent. The figure is also similar by age—70 percent for workers 25 to 34 and for workers 55 to 59. The results differ by earnings, however. For those earning $5,000-$9,999, 43 percent with prior pension coverage were currently covered. The percentage was twice that, 86 percent, for workers earning more than $50,000. The figures also vary greatly by industry, 84 percent in manufacturing and 54 percent in retail trade. The figures vary greatly by size of current employer. For workers in firms with 25 or fewer workers, 29 percent with prior pension coverage were currently covered, versus 89 percent for workers in firms with 250 or more workers.

TYPES OF PORTABILITY LOSS

Pension benefits are lost due to job change for three reasons: (1) workers change jobs before vesting; (2) plans provide lower benefits per year of service for job leavers; or (3) job leavers cash out their pensions and spend the money.

Vesting Losses

A worker with a vested pension is guaranteed to receive the nominal value of those funds at retirement. Thus, when a worker who is fully vested in pension benefits worth $100 a month quits, he/she will receive $100 a month at retirement. When the worker is 50 percent vested, he/she will receive $50 a month. Workers who are not vested receive nothing.

Before the Employee Retirement Income Security Act of 1974 (ERISA), federal law did not set minimum years for vesting. Many pension plans vested workers' rights to benefits after they had reached age 45 and had 15 years of service. This meant that a worker with many years of service could be laid off or change jobs and receive no pension.

In passing ERISA, Congress wished to ensure that long-service pension-covered workers would receive their retirement benefits. Prior

Table 4.1
Pension Coverage Rates on Current and Prior Jobs, 1988

Worker characteristics	Workers (thousands)	Current participants[a]			Prior participants (%)	Current[a] and prior participants (%)	Current[a] or prior participants (%)
		Total (%)	Defined benefit[b] (%)	Defined contribution[b] (%)			
Total	72,491	48	28	9	18	10	56
Sex							
Male	43,491	50	30	10	20	11	59
Female	29,000	43	25	9	15	7	51
Race							
White	63,403	48	29	10	19	10	57
Black	7,011	42	26	6	13	7	48
Other	2,078	48	28	8	11	6	54
Earnings							
$1-$4,999	2,168	7	5	1	12	1	18
$5,000-$9,999	8,085	15	7	3	11	2	24
$10,000-$14,999	13,542	35	19	8	13	5	43
$15,000-$19,999	11,388	49	27	11	17	9	57
$20,000-$24,999	9,648	60	38	10	18	10	68
$25,000-$29,999	6,742	68	42	12	23	14	77
$30,000-$49,999	11,369	74	47	13	25	17	81
$50,000 or more	3,465	79	48	16	33	27	85
Not reported	6,085	24	10	6	15	4	34

Table 4.1 (continued)

Worker characteristics	Workers (thousands)	Current participants[a]			Prior participants (%)	Current[a] and prior participants (%)	Current[a] or prior participants (%)
		Total (%)	Defined benefit[b] (%)	Defined contribution[b] (%)			
Age							
16-20	3,429	12	6	2	2	1	13
21-24	7,837	26	14	5	6	2	31
25-34	24,476	46	26	11	15	8	54
35-44	17,788	56	34	11	24	14	67
45-54	11,476	58	37	10	23	13	68
55-59	4,040	57	39	7	21	12	67
60-64	2,385	55	39	8	27	14	68
65 or older	1,060	33	18	6	26	7	52
Occupation							
Professional/ technical	9,494	60	34	13	24	15	69
Managers/officials	10,285	56	31	12	25	15	66
Sales	8,388	40	21	8	21	10	51
Administrative support	11,067	51	31	11	17	9	60
Craftsmen	11,061	52	34	10	16	9	60
Operatives	7,223	53	36	7	10	5	58
Transportation equipment operator	3,617	44	27	9	19	8	55

Nonfarm laborers	3,332	36	23	6	10	5	41
Service workers	6,656	22	11	4	11	4	29
Other	1,417	13	6	4	8	2	19
Tenure							
Less than 1 year	12,853	16	7	3	23	7	32
1-4 years	24,952	38	19	10	21	11	48
5-9 years	12,693	62	36	13	18	13	67
10-14 years	7,840	72	47	13	13	10	74
15 years or more	11,131	78	56	10	9	7	80
Not reported	3,023	23	11	2	15	6	33
Union status[c]							
Union	10,283	78	57	9	14	11	81
Nonunion	56,810	44	25	10	19	10	53
Not reported	5,398	25	11	6	15	4	36
Firm size							
Fewer than 25	16,784	16	7	4	15	3	28
25-99	9,804	35	17	10	19	8	47
100-249	5,637	47	23	12	18	10	56
250 or more	34,248	68	45	11	19	14	74
Not reported	6,019	36	18	7	16	7	44

SOURCE: May 1988 Current Population Survey; Piacentini (1990b).

a. A worker is considered to be a current pension participant if he or she reported inclusion in a pension, retirement, profit sharing, stock, or 401(k)-type plan at a wage and salary job, or reported a secondary self-employed job and contributions to an IRA or Keogh.

b. A large degree of response error may be present in worker responses on plan type. See discussion of this issue in this paper.

c. Workers are classified as union if they reported union membership or coverage under a union contract.

Table 4.2
Pension Coverage of Workers Covered on a Prior Job

Worker characteristics	Participant at any prior job (thousands)	Proportion currently covered[b] (%)	Proportion currently participating[a]			
			Total (%)	Defined benefit[c] (%)	Defined contribution[c] (%)	Plan type not reported (%)
Total	12,998	69	53	30	12	12
Sex						
Male	8,706	70	56	32	13	12
Female	4,292	67	47	24	11	12
Race						
White	11,850	69	53	30	13	11
Black	915	71	51	29	8	14
Other	232	73	53	32	[d]	21
Earnings						
$1-$4,999	270	25	9	9	[d]	[d]
$5,000-$9,999	887	43	16	6	4	5
$10,000-$14,999	1,792	57	35	17	7	11
$15,000-$19,999	1,909	70	52	25	13	13
$20,000-$24,999	1,773	71	55	33	12	10
$25,000-$29,999	1,530	79	63	39	12	11
$30,000-$49,999	2,787	84	71	40	16	15
$50,000 or more	1,150	86	81	48	19	14
Not reported	900	40	29	12	8	9

	Number					
Age						
16-20	81	79	42	37	d	5
21-24	496	49	25	15	3	7
25-34	3,766	70	51	26	15	9
35-44	4,226	73	58	32	13	13
45-54	2,655	68	57	32	12	12
55-59	868	70	54	32	7	15
60-64	632	66	54	39	4	12
65 or older	273	47	26	12	5	9
Industry						
Agriculture	90	38	28	15	8	5
Manufacturing						
Total	3,550	84	67	40	12	15
Nondurable	1,394	79	60	37	9	13
Durable	2,155	88	72	42	14	16
Trade						
Total	2,383	57	41	20	11	9
Wholesale	847	63	52	26	13	13
Retail	1,536	54	34	17	10	7
Services						
Total	3,354	62	44	19	14	11
Professional	2,176	68	48	21	15	12
Business and personal	1,178	50	37	16	10	10
Transportation	591	60	50	33	9	8

Table 4.2 (continued)

Worker characteristics	Participant at any prior job (thousands)	Proportion currently covered[b] (%)	Proportion currently participating[a]			
			Total (%)	Defined benefit[c] (%)	Defined contribution[c] (%)	Plan type not reported (%)
Communication and utilities	418	87	74	58	10	6
Construction	850	48	41	22	11	7
Finance, insurance, and real estate	1,581	79	61	35	12	14
Mining	181	74	60	41	5	14
Tenure						
Less than 1 year	2,950	59	30	15	6	8
1-4 years	5,305	66	50	24	14	12
5-9 years	2,274	78	72	44	17	12
10-14 years	1,010	82	78	50	12	16
15 years or more	994	82	78	53	12	12
Not reported	466	63	37	20	3	14
Union status[e]						
Union	1,446	91	78	53	12	13
Nonunion	10,718	68	52	28	12	12
Not reported	833	40	29	12	9	9
Firm size						
Fewer than 25	2,559	29	21	8	8	6

25-99	1,868	55	41	18	13	10
100-249	1,018	71	53	24	15	14
250 or more	6,618	89	70	43	14	14
Not reported	936	64	48	24	11	13

SOURCE: May 1988 Current Population Survey; Piacentini (1990b).

a. A worker is considered to be a current pension participant if he or she reported inclusion in a pension retirement, profit sharing, stock, or 401(k)-type plan at a wage and salary job, or reported a secondary self-employed job and contributions to an IRA or Keogh.

b. A worker is considered to be currently covered by a pension if his or her employer sponsored a pension, retirement, profit-sharing, stock, or 401(k)-type plan for any employees, or if he or she reported a secondary self-employed job and contributions to an IRA or Keogh.

c. A large degree of response error may be present in worker responses on plan type. See discussion of this issue in this paper.

d. No observations in category.

e. Workers are classified as union if they reported union membership or coverage under a union contract.

to 1989, ERISA required private pension plans to at least partially vest after 10 years.[3] Most plans offered 10-year cliff vesting, with zero vesting up to 10 years, and then 100 percent vesting after that plateau. Starting in 1989, ERISA required firms to at least partially vest workers after five years in single-employer pension plans, which cover about 90 percent of participants. Most single-employer defined benefit plans now offer five-year cliff vesting. Workers with less than five years of tenure lose all rights to benefits under these plans, and firms offering cliff vesting can thus avoid paying pension benefits for short-term workers. By law, worker contributions vest immediately.

Plan Design Losses

Fully vested workers in defined benefit plans still lose retirement benefits when changing jobs due to the ways employers design pension benefit formulas.

Defined Benefit Plans

Under defined benefit plans, employers figure benefits using various earnings and service formulas (table 4.3), and losses vary with each plan design.

Final-pay benefit formulas are the most common defined benefit plans. In 1989, 64 percent of enrolled workers in large and medium-sized firms were enrolled in final-pay defined benefit plans.

Between the time a vested worker leaves and the time a plan begins paying benefits, the fixed nominal benefit declines in real value due to inflation. Consider a worker earning $25,000 leaving a job at age 45 with 10 years of service. Under a defined benefit plan, his/her vested benefit might be 1 percent of final salary times the number of years of service. Thus, the vested annual pension benefit, which a worker could begin collecting in this plan at age 65, is $2,500 a year (figured as .01 x $25,000 x 10 years of service).

If the same worker had worked under the plan from age 55 to 65, rather than from 45 to 55, he/she would receive much higher benefits for 10 years of work. If the worker's income only kept pace with inflation, and if inflation were 4 percent a year, the salary at 65 would be $55,000. Thus, the annual retirement benefit from the plan would be $5,500.

Table 4.3
Benefit Formulas in Defined Benefit Plans, 1989
(percent of full-time participants)

Basis of payment[a]	All participants	Professional and administrative participants	Technical and clerical participants	Production and service participants
Total	100	100	100	100
Terminal earnings formula	64	77	76	51
No alternative formula	35	42	45	25
Terminal earnings alternative	10	11	9	10
Career-earnings alternative	3	4	4	2
Dollar-amount alternative[b]	17	20	18	14
Percent of contributions alternative	c	c	c	—
Career-earnings formula	11	15	10	10
No alternative formula	6	8	7	4
Career-earnings alternative	c	c	c	1
Dollar-amount alternative[b]	5	7	3	5
Dollar-amount formula[b]	22	6	11	37
No alternative formula	19	5	9	32
Dollar-amount alternative[b]	2	1	2	3
Percent of contributions alternative	1	c	c	1
Percent of contributions formula	1	c	c	2
Cash account	2	2	3	1

SOURCE: U.S. Department of Labor (1990).
NOTES: Excludes supplemental pension plans. Because of rounding, sums of individual items may not equal totals. Dash indicates no employees in this category.
a. Alternative formulas are generally designed to provide a minimum benefit for employees with short service or low earnings.
b. Includes formulas based on dollar amounts for each year of service and flat monthly benefit varying by service.
c. Less than 0.5 percent.

This worker has the same real earnings (adjusted for inflation) and the same tenure. But work between ages 55 and 65 yielded a benefit worth over twice that earned between ages 35 and 45. The two retirement benefits differ because the plan did not index the salary used in figuring the job leaver's benefit. Inflation between ages 45 and 65 cuts the real value of the wages used to figure the benefit.

The worker also would have earned over twice the benefit per year for the earlier 10-year period had he/she continued working with the same employer until age 65. This follows because the benefit earned during that decade also would have been figured using the $55,000 final earnings. The worker lost 55 percent of pension benefits for work from age 35 to 45 that he/she would have earned had he/she worked until retirement.

This illustrates that even moderate inflation, like that experienced during the early 1990s, causes large portability losses for workers covered by final-pay benefit formulas. Other sources of wage growth—general productivity growth, promotion, and merit pay raises—cause added portability loss. With a 4 percent annual increase due to inflation and a 1.5 percent annual increase due to productivity growth, the worker's salary at age 65 is $75,000 In this case, the worker loses 66 percent of the benefits he/she would have received for the earlier period had he/she stayed with the employer until retirement.

Benefit losses are even larger than those losses due to wage growth in plans where the eligibility age for full retirement benefits depends on minimum service (Gustman and Steinmeier 1989a). These plans reward continuing employment by lowering or removing the penalty for early retirement and by crediting extra service and higher salary when figuring benefits.

Plans based on a *career-average benefit formula* covered 11 percent of workers in defined benefit plans in large and medium-sized firms in 1989. Workers in these plans would appear to maintain benefits when changing jobs because the pension benefit is figured as a share of average (nominal) pay over the worker's career. Such plans count pay earned each year with the employer; therefore, job change would appear not to affect the value of benefits accrued to date.

In career-average plans, however, preretirement inflation erodes the real value of benefits. Erosion occurs equally for those who leave and those who stay until retirement. While final earnings generally keep pace with inflation, earlier earnings, which are fixed in nominal terms, do not. Inflation lowers the real value of the career-average salary because nominal earnings are used to compute the career average.

To counteract inflationary loss, most employers periodically update the career-average earnings base, amending the plan to raise pay bases in order to counteract the effect of inflation. Typically, employers adjust the base only for workers they employ as of the adjustment date. Thus, job leavers in career-average plans suffer portability losses because they do not benefit from subsequent pay adjustments used for benefit calculation.

Collectively bargained plans, negotiated between management and labor, generally figure benefits as a flat sum per year of service. In 1989, 22 percent of workers in defined benefit plans in medium-size and large firms were covered by *flat-dollar benefit formulas.*

In a flat-dollar plan, a retiring worker might receive a monthly benefit of $18 times years of service. If the worker had worked 30 years under the pension plan, the monthly benefit would be $540.

It might appear that job leavers do not lose benefits in this type of plan. The dollars per year of service would be the same for those who leave and those who stay. But employers typically raise the dollar units (per year of service) used in calculating benefits each time they renegotiate the union contract. Job leavers in this type of plan lose benefits because former workers who have not reached retirement age rarely share in the dollar unit increases.

In sum, even though some defined benefit pension formulas do not explicitly adjust for final earnings, most do in practice. This results in pension benefit losses for job leavers, because they have relatively low final earnings and lose benefits primarily due to inflation. During inflationary periods, creditors lose and debtors gain when assets are fixed in nominal terms. Job leavers who were enrolled in defined benefit plans on prior jobs are creditors with assets fixed in nominal terms. They lose.

Defined Contribution Plans

Under a defined contribution plan, the employer, the worker, or both contribute. The plan credits contributions and investment earnings to an employee account where workers' contributions vest immediately. When an employee has worked long enough for the employer's contributions to vest, the account balance plus all future earnings provide retirement income for the worker, even if he/she changes jobs. Most defined contribution plans treat short- and long-term workers equally; thus, vested short-term workers do not lose benefits when changing jobs if they leave the money with the plan. However, job leavers in some defined contribution plans do lose benefits due to backloading. In these plans, the employer contributes a higher percentage of pay for long-service workers.[4]

Losses Due to Preretirement Distributions

Fully vested job leavers may lose retirement benefits if they receive a lump sum cash distribution from their pension plan. Employers with defined benefit plans figure lump sum payments according to actuarial tables the employer chooses with the plan actuary's advice (within limits set by the federal government). Under defined contribution plans, the distributed lump sum is the amount of money in the worker's retirement account.

Employers who cash out terminating workers sidestep administrative burdens and are not required to pay the yearly premiums to the Pension Benefit Guaranty Corporation (PBGC). In 1992 those premiums ranged from $19 to $72 per participant in defined benefit plans, with underfunded plans charged the higher rates by PBGC. Typically, plans pay lump sum distributions directly to the job leaver, who then has several options. He/she can (1) spend the money, (2) transfer it to another tax-qualified pension arrangement such as an IRA, or (3) save it in a nonretirement account.

If the worker spends the distribution, it provides no retirement benefits. If the worker transfers the money to another tax-qualified arrangement or saves it in a nonretirement account, he/she can use the sum for retirement. Saving it in a tax-qualified retirement account yields a higher return because the worker benefits from tax preferences.

In the three cases, however, the job leaver loses benefits if the distribution is from a defined benefit plan, due to the benefit being calculated using termination rather than retirement age wages. Also, when taking a lump sum cashout, the worker surrenders the survivor protection and *ad hoc* cost-of-living increases that a defined benefit plan might have paid.

The Tax Reform Act of 1986 requires plans to figure lump sum distributions for small and medium-sized amounts using the Pension Benefit Guaranty Corporation interest rate for calculating deferred liabilities. Because this rate is less than a market rate, workers will receive a generous lump sum. This generosity prompts workers to take lump sum distributions.[5] However, for large distributions the firm may use an interest rate closer to a market rate.

If job leavers take a lump sum distribution and roll over the money into an IRA, they may lose benefits even from a defined contribution. First, individuals tend to invest conservatively. Second, employers sometimes pay plan administrative expenses rather than charging them against plan assets; the individual bears the expenses of an IRA. Third, economies of scale make administering an employer plan less costly than an individual plan. Fourth, employer plans can invest in large denomination securities with a better rate of return. Individual IRAs have too few assets to make investing in large denomination securities feasible.

Workers who are not changing jobs may also incur losses from preretirement distributions. A worker may be eligible for a preretirement hardship withdrawal from a defined contribution plan. The IRS allows this exception for unreimbursed medical expenses, purchase of a principal residence, educational expenses, and prevention of eviction/foreclosure. Hardship withdrawals cut future retirement benefits, but are not a portability loss because the employee has remained with the company.

A worker whose firm or division is sold also may receive a distribution without changing jobs.[6] In 1986 the IRS took the "same desk" position: if an employee leaves work Friday and returns Monday to the same desk but is working for a different employer, he/she cannot claim a distribution from the pension plan. In 1990, the IRS changed its mind.[7] Now the employee may take a distribution of benefits in the same desk scenario if the old employer permits it, unless pension assets and liabilities transfer to the new employer. The decision enables employers to control whether they will make preretirement distributions. If the pension assets and liabilities are not transferred to the purchaser, preretirement distributions arising from the sale are allowed.

Distributions to affected workers are now allowed for stock sales of businesses. In a stock sale, the worker's corporate employer stays the same, though corporate employer ownership changes. The employment relationship with the employer maintaining the plan is severed if, among other conditions, the pension plan is maintained by the original parent but is no longer maintained by the subsidiary in the new owner's hands.

HOW IMPORTANT ARE PORTABILITY LOSSES?

The size of portability losses has been examined by an actuarial consulting firm, Hay/Huggins Incorporated (1988), under contract to the U.S. Department of Labor. To do this, they derived job mobility patterns from the Survey of Consumer Finances (SCF), which includes extensive pension and job tenure data. Workers with differing lifetime job mobility patterns were assigned pension coverage based on coverage data by pension plan type.

The Hay/Huggins study used a simplified model of U.S. career patterns and pension plans, including only primary plan coverage. (About 40 percent of pension-covered workers are also covered by a supplementary defined contribution plan (Turner and Beller 1992).) Workers initially enrolled in a pension plan were assumed to have coverage on all successive jobs. Thus, workers with career gaps in pension coverage were not considered. The simulation used a five-year cliff-vesting rule for all plans. (While most single-employer plans use five-year cliff vesting, multiemployer plans commonly use 10-year cliff vesting.) The study estimated expected portability losses caused by pension coverage patterns for representative job histories.

Ignoring preretirement cashouts of pension benefits, pensioners lose, on average, 15 percent of lifetime benefits they would have earned if all pension-covered work had fallen under the last pension plan in which they were enrolled (table 4.4). This figure applies to all pension-covered workers, including those who do not change jobs. It considers portability loss due to failure to vest completely and failure to index deferred vested benefits.

The percentage loss figure is for primary plans only and ignores social security and secondary private pension plans. As social security causes no portability loss, including social security benefits reduces the portability loss to 10 percent of retirement benefits. Because secondary plans are typically portable defined contribution plans, including them would indicate that the percentage of all retirement benefits workers lose due to vesting and plan design is smaller. However, because of the lump sum option for terminating workers in defined contribution plans, to include supplementary plans probably would raise the portability loss relative to benefits.

Table 4.4
Loss in Portability Model

Percentage of benefits as portability loss	Percentage of covered workers
40-49	6.3
30-39	13.4
20-29	19.4
10-19	15.2
1-9	4.6
None	38.4
Gain	2.7
Total	100.0
Average loss for all workers	14.8
Average loss for workers with a loss	23.3

SOURCE: Hay/Huggins (1988).
NOTE: The portability loss is the percentage difference between the retirement benefit the worker would have received if all service had been covered by the retirement plan of the last employer and the benefit that the worker actually received. A worker who worked from at least age 30 to age 65 under one pension plan would not have a loss under this definition since the maximum credited service for the plans in the model was 35 years. A worker who worked for 35 years under one plan and received a vested benefit from a second plan would show a "gain."

Of pension-covered workers, 41 percent suffered no portability loss. They either stayed with the same employer for 35 or more years and then retired, or they were covered by primary defined contribution plans (considered in the study to cause no portability losses). The 59 percent of pension-covered workers who did suffer portability loss, on average lost 23 percent of retirement income.

While 5 percent of workers losing benefits lost less than 10 percent of their benefits, 6 percent lost between 40 and 49 percent of their benefits. In 1988 dollars, workers losing benefits lost, on average, $5,000 of future annual income per year of retirement.

Portability losses are higher for pension-covered workers with multiple job changes (table 4.5). Workers with one job change lost 10 percent, those with two changes lost 20 percent, and those with three changes lost, on average, 25 percent of the benefits they would have received had they stayed with one employer.

Table 4.5
Portability Loss by Number of Jobs

Number of jobs	Percentage loss
1	0.0
2	10.0
3	13.9
4	21.3
5	24.4
6	31.1
7	42.4

SOURCE: Hay/Huggins (1988).

Losses also vary by plan type (table 4.6). Workers covered by multiemployer and defined contribution plans have little, if any, loss regardless of how many times they change jobs. They lose benefits in those plans primarily because they move before vesting. (Job leavers in multiemployer plans were assumed to go to another employer in the same multiemployer plan.) Workers who were covered by single-employer defined benefit plans and who changed jobs had losses from 16 to 24 percent, depending on plan type. Those who suffered the highest losses were enrolled in final-salary plans

Table 4.6
Portability Loss by Type of Plan

Type of plan	Percentage loss
Multiemployer	1.5
Flat-dollar	16.1
Final-pay	
Offset	24.6
Step rate	23.8
Career-average	18.1
Defined contribution	1.0

SOURCE: Hay/Huggins (1988).

Preretirement Distributions

Evidence suggests that portability losses due to preretirement lump sum distributions are growing because these distributions are becoming more common. Of the 8.5 million civilian workers in May 1988 reporting a lump sum distribution from a prior job's plan, 4.4 million indicated that they had received a distribution since 1983 (Piacentini 1990b). A total of 1.1 million workers reported having received multiple distributions. Between 1983 and 1988, the share of workers who reported having received a lump sum distribution from a prior job rose from 6.6 to 7.5 percent. In May 1988, 21.6 million nonfarm workers— 21 percent—reported being eligible for a lump sum distribution from the primary retirement plan at a current job.

Hay/Huggins estimated that average portability losses of covered workers would rise from 15 to 39 percent if job leavers cashed out all vested benefits from primary plans. But they estimated that only 25 percent of primary plans allowed cashouts of $3,500 or more. If workers consumed all lump sum distributions available, the average employee would lose 21 percent, instead of the 15 percent now attributed to inflation and failure to vest.   Thus, Hay/Huggins estimated, 25 percent of portability losses are due to workers consuming lump sum benefits before retirement. The U.S. Department of Labor, by including supplemental defined contribution plans, estimates that lump sum distributions are, in fact, much larger. The DOL suggests that these distributions constitute two-thirds of the portability losses incurred (Ball 1990).

Projecting Portability Loss

In deciding how to cut portability loss, policymakers must consider the future. If workers are expected to lose little in the future, then the need for portability diminishes.[8] Projecting pension benefit losses is speculative, but nonetheless may aid policymakers in deciding what types of portability policies to pursue.

Table 4.7 contains projected portability loss to the year 2000. A straight line projection of the shift from defined benefit to defined contribution plans is used. The 15 percent portability loss in 1987 falls to 9 percent by the year 2000.

Table 4.7
Projection of Portability Loss to the Year 2000

	1987 defined benefit/ defined contribution mix (%)	Year 2000 defined benefit/ defined contribution mix (%)
Primary Benefit	14.7	9.0
Primary + Supplemental*		8.0
Primary + Supplemental* + Social Security		6.1

SOURCE: Hay/Huggins (1988).
*Assumes 90 percent of employees covered by single employer primary defined benefit plan have a supplemental defined contribution plan.

Including supplemental defined contribution plans and social security permits figuring the share of total retirement benefits lost to job change. The projections indicate that by the year 2000 workers will lose 6 percent of their total retirement benefits due to job change. This estimate excludes preretirement lump sum payments, the subject of the next chapter.

NOTES

1. This calculation is based on the worker's expected salary at retirement. The worker's expected benefits at normal retirement age, early retirement age, and the age that maximizes the present value of benefits all may affect his/her expected retirement age.

2. Final salary refers to final average salary, often the average of the workers highest five years of salary.

3. Years of participation in a pension plan do not necessarily equal years of work for an employer. However, later in the text, the term "years of work" is used rather than the more technically precise term "years of participation."

4. In the past, a portability loss was suffered in some defined contribution plans due to class-year vesting, which is no longer permitted. With class-year vesting, regardless of the number of years of service, an employer's contributions for the current year did not vest until a later year.

5. To determine the value of the lump sum payment, an interest rate is used to discount future benefits.

6. This section draws on material presented in Wyatt (1990).

7. In a general counsel memorandum discussed in Chernoff (1990, p. 18).

8. This section is based on "Projection of Total Portability Loss," a report by Hay/Huggins to the Department of Labor, February 1991.

5

Preretirement Use
of Retirement Benefits

Workers cashing out their pension plans when they change jobs is the major cause of lost retirement benefits. The practice has raised concern that the current generation of workers will have insufficient retirement income when it retires. This chapter examines who cashes out and how much they receive.[1] Two U.S. Bureau of the Census surveys provide data on these preretirement lump sum distributions: the May 1983 Current Population Survey Pension Supplement (CPS PS) and the May 1988 Current Population Survey Employee Benefit Supplement (CPS EBS). Each of these surveys included questions about receipt and use of lump sum distributions by civilian workers.

The chapter begins by providing a framework for discussion of preretirement lump sum distributions. It is followed by more detailed examinations of the availability, receipt, and use of the distributions as reflected in the 1983 and 1988 CPS pension supplements.

BACKGROUND

The growth of defined contribution plans as primary retirement options and as supplemental plans has increased the availability and receipt of preretirement lump sum distributions. Unlike defined benefit plans, defined contribution plans typically pay lump sum distributions at retirement or preretirement job separation. The trend toward defined contribution plans coincides with enactment of the Employee Retirement Income Security Act of 1974 (ERISA), which provides a convenient reference point. Total active participants in defined contribution plans increased from 9.8 million in 1975, before ERISA fully took effect, to 27.5 million in 1987—a 281 percent increase. Active participants in defined benefit plans increased only 6 percent over the same period, gaining 1.5 million for a total of 28.0 million participants in 1987.

ERISA permits defined benefit plans to cash out job leavers with small accrued benefits, set at a maximum of $3,500, without requiring consent of the participants. Laws regulating pensions enacted since ERISA continue to permit lump sum distributions, at the same time discouraging workers from consuming cashouts by imposing excise taxes or other economic disincentives.

With the Tax Reform Act (TRA) of 1986, Congress mandated several changes to encourage workers to save distributions for retirement. It imposed a 10 percent excise tax on all preretirement distributions from qualified retirement plans, including Individual Retirement Accounts (IRAs). This tax does not apply to distributions rolled over to another qualified plan, to an IRA, or to distributions of employee contributions.

In another move inducing workers not to cash out, Congress, in the TRA, repealed 10-year forward averaging and substituted one-time 5-year tax averaging for a lump sum distribution after the individual has reached age 59 1/2. The TRA also phased out, over six years, the long-term capital gains tax treatment of lump sum distributions. In 1992 Congress imposed a 20 percent withholding on lump sum distributions that were not rolled over.

LUMP SUM DISTRIBUTIONS

Availability

Data show substantial availability of lump sum distributions before retirement, with the greater proportion available from defined contribution plans. Using May 1988 data, Piacentini (1990b) finds that one-fifth of full-time private sector wage and salary workers reported current eligibility to receive a preretirement lump sum distribution from their primary retirement plan.

Recipients in 1983

In 1983, 6.6 million currently employed workers reported receiving a lump sum from a prior employer's pension or capital accumulation plan at some time. This means that three out of every five workers who had changed jobs and were vested in the prior employer's plan took a lump sum distribution upon job change (Atkins 1986).

Definite patterns emerge in analysis of the 6.6 million recipients (table 5.1). One-half of the men and three-quarters of the women who were vested in a previous plan took a lump sum upon job change. Among age groups, younger workers had the highest percentages of lump sum receipt, with workers between ages 25 and 34 showing the highest rate (76 percent). Workers in the ascending age groups that follow show a pattern of decreasing lump sum receipt through the 65 and over age group, which had only a 21 percent rate of receipt.

Receipt by income level shows consistency in the four middle ranges covering between $5,000 and $30,000. These four categories show rates of lump sum receipt ranging from 62 to 64 percent. Workers earning less than $5,000 had the highest rates of lump sum receipt (71 percent), and those earning $50,000 or more had the lowest (46 percent).

Regarding the amount of the distribution, although a greater percentage of women than men took a lump sum upon job change, they also more commonly received smaller amounts than men. Eighty-four percent of workers received a lump sum of less than $5,000, and only 8 percent of women received $5,000 or more versus 20 percent of men (table 5.2). While these amounts appear small, it should be remembered that they would be considerably larger if left in the plan until retirement. At 3 percent real interest, a lump sum distribution of $5,000 taken at age 30 would grow to $14,300 in real dollars at age 65. Among other characteristics, age and income had the greatest association with lump sum distribution amounts. Older workers and high-income individuals received the largest amounts.

Table 5.1
Percentage of Workers with a Pension from a Previous Job Receiving
a Lump Sum by Characteristic of Worker, 1983

Worker characteristics	Received lump sum (%)	Total (thousands)
Sex		
Male	50.9	7,033
Female	76.7	3,902
Age		
Under 25	51.2	319
25–34	75.5	2,867
35–44	68.9	3,091
45–54	54.8	2,285
55–64	41.5	1,781
65 or over	20.9	590
Income		
Missing	57.5	489
$0 or negative	44.1	139
$1–$4,999	71.3	753
$5,000–$9,999	63.9	1,338
$10,000–$14,999	61.0	1,882
$15,000–$19,999	63.2	1,704
$20,000–$29,999	61.7	2,356
$30,000–$49,999	52.4	1,594
$50,000 or more	45.6	676
Total	60.1	10,935

SOURCE: Data from Atkins (1986).

Table 5.2
Amount of Lump Sum Received by Characteristic of Worker, 1983

Worker characteristics	Received less than $5,000 (%)	Received $5,000 and over (%)	Don't know (%)	Total (thousands)
Sex				
Male	78.3	19.9	1.8	3,580
Female	91.1	8.2	0.7	2,993
Age				
Under 25	99.5	0.5	0.0	163
25–34	91.9	7.0	1.1	2,164
35–44	83.7	15.6	0.7	2,130
45–54	78.9	18.9	2.2	1,253
55–64	71.2	26.4	2.4	739
65 or over	67.6	32.4	0.0	123
Income				
Missing	84.7	12.0	3.3	282
$0 or negative	57.8	37.5	4.7	61
$1–$4,999	91.1	6.7	2.2	537
$5,000–$9,999	91.7	7.3	1.0	855
$10,000–$14,999	89.1	10.4	0.5	1,147
$15,000–$19,999	85.4	14.3	0.3	1,076
$20,000–$29,999	84.7	13.4	1.9	1,453
$30,000–$49,999	73.5	24.8	1.6	835
$50,000 or more	62.2	37.4	0.4	308
Total	84.3	14.5	1.3	6,574

SOURCE: Data from Atkins (1986).
NOTE: Numbers may not add to 100 due to rounding.

Uses in 1983

Analysis of the 1983 CPS pension data shows that the uses of preretirement lump sums are strongly associated with the dollar amount. Only 26 percent of those receiving distributions of less than $5,000 saved some of the money (table 5.3). This percentage more than doubles for the $5,000 to $9,999 distribution range (58 percent), rises to 79 percent in the $10,000 to $19,000 range, and peaks at 87 percent in the $20,000 and over range. The greatest number of recipients, 84 percent, received less than $5,000, and 77 percent of these spent some or all of the sum. The $5,000 to $9,999 category had the next highest number of recipients, 9 percent, and 52 percent of these spent some or all of the sum.

Defining retirement savings to include only rollover of the lump sum into another tax-qualified retirement vehicle, an IRA, or a tax-deferred annuity, only recipients of large lump sums who were either older or college educated had high rates of retirement savings (Atkins 1986). Andrews (1985) calculated that 4.4 percent of recipients save for retirement in this way (table 5.3).

Recipients in 1988

The May 1988 CPS pension supplement showed that there were 20 million civilian workers age 16 and over who reported participating in a private pension or retirement plan at a prior job (Piacentini 1990b). The workers reporting a lump sum distribution from a prior employer's plan increased to 8.5 million in 1988 from the 6.6 million in 1983 when there were 16.9 million workers reporting coverage by a pension in a previous job. This increase in number of recipients is an increase in the percentage of employees participating in a prior employer's plan who reported receiving a lump sum (39 and 43 percent). The average amount of the sum in real terms did not change substantially over time. Distributions received after 1984 in constant 1988 dollars averaged $8,300, versus $7,700 for 1975-79, and $6,600 for 1960-69.

In 1988, 60 percent of lump sums were received before age 35, and 85 percent were received before age 45, perhaps because most job changes occur at younger ages (table 5.4). This pattern resembles that shown in 1983 data. The change in preretirement lump sum distribution between 1983 and 1988 when examined by characteristics of recipients is no more than 5 percent in almost every category under gender, age, and income. The 1983 and 1988 sets of lump sum recipients closely resemble each other when distribution is compared according to the characteristics of the workers (table 5.5).

Although small lump sums are a relatively low percentage of the total dollar amount of distributions, they represent most of the distributions. Of the total amount distributed in preretirement lump sum distributions, 8 percent are in amounts of less than $2,500 and 17 percent are distributed in amounts of less than $5,000 (table 5.4). At the same time, one-half of lump sum recipients receive payments of less than

Table 5.3
Use of Preretirement Lump Sum Distributions by Purpose and Amount, 1983

	Total	Less than $5,000	$5,000–$9,999	$10,000–$19,999	$20,000 and over
Total recipients[a] (thousands)	6,594	5,534	583	219	154
Percentage distribution[a]	100.0	84.2	8.9	3.3	2.3
Percentage all uses[b]	100.0	100.0	100.0	100.0	100.0
Total saving	32.0	26.2	57.6	78.9	87.3
Retirement program	4.4	2.4	c	c	c
Insurance annuity	c	c	c	c	c
Housing purchase	10.1	9.3	12.5	c	c
Other investment	16.8	14.0	29.9	45.9	c
Total consumption	71.4	76.6	51.9	42.6	c
Car purchase	4.8	4.8	c	c	c
Vacation	3.2	3.1	c	c	c
Other use	63.4	68.7	40.9	c	c

SOURCE: Andrews (1985, p. 163).

a. Recipients by lump sum amount are less than total recipients and percentages are less than 100 percent because of the omission of "don't know" and "no response" to value of distribution.

b. Percentages may add to more than 100 percent because recipients may have used lump sum distribution in more than one way.

c. Number of workers too small for rates to be calculated reliably.

$2,500. Those receiving less than $5,000 are 70 percent of total recipients. Thus, allowing workers to cash out amounts of $5,000 or less would not affect 70 percent of workers receiving distributions, but would preserve most of the pension money taken in lump sum distributions until retirement.

Uses in 1988

The increase in the rollover of distributions into tax-qualified vehicles is one of the chief findings from the 1988 data. The 4.4 percent of recipients reported to have used some of the distribution for a retirement program or tax deferred annuity in 1983 under the narrowest definition of savings (Andrews 1985) increased to 13 percent in 1988.

The May 1983 and May 1988 CPS benefit supplements cannot be compared exactly on lump sum use because the two sets of recipients were asked different questions. The high number of recipients—63 percent—indicating the "other" uses category in 1983 prompted a change in the 1988 questionnaire in order to target these uses in more detail. The effort successfully reduced the other uses choice to 27 percent in 1988. The following lists compare the two sets of options concerning use of any part of the recipient's distribution.

1983	**1988**
• Invested in a retirement program	• Invested in an IRA
	• Invested in an insurance annuity or other retirement program
• Invested in an insurance annuity	
• Invested in other financial instruments	• Invested in other financial instruments
	• Put into a savings account
	• Started or purchased a business
• Bought a house	• Bought a house or paid a mortgage
• Bought a car	• Bought a car
• Went on vacation	
	• Paid off loans or other debts
	• Paid educational expenses for self or others
	• Paid expenses during a period of unemployment
• Other uses	• Other uses

Table 5.4
Distribution of Amount of Lump Sum (LS) Payments, 1983

Worker characteristics	Recipients		Aggregate amount[a]		Average amount per recipient[d]
	(thousands)[b]	Percentage of total[c]	(billions)[b]	Percentage of total[c]	
Total	$8,478	100	$48.1	100	$6,800
Amount of most recent LS					
$1–$499	1,042	15	0.3	1	300
$500–$999	955	13	0.7	1	700
$1,000–$2,499	1,627	23	2.7	6	1,200
$2,500–$4,999	1,220	17	4.4	9	3,600
$5,000–$9,999	1,114	16	7.9	16	7,100
$10,000–$14,999	449	6	5.4	11	12,000
$15,000–$19,999	211	3	3.6	7	16,900
$20,000–$49,999	335	5	9.7	20	29,100
$50,000 or more	160	2	13.5	28	67,200
Year in which most recent LS was received					
1985–1988[a]	3,391	41	19.7	41	6,500
1980–1984	2,403	29	13.8	29	6,600
1975–1979	1,191	14	7.5	16	7,700
1970–1974	579	7	3.4	7	7,200

Table 5.4 (continued)
Distribution of Amount of Lump Sum (LS) Payments, 1983

Worker characteristics	Recipients		Aggregate amount[a]		Average amount per recipient[d]
	(thousands)[b]	Percentage of total[c]	(billions)[b]	Percentage of total[c]	
1960–1969	558	7	2.7	6	6,600
Before 1960	156	2	0.5	1	5,400
Sex					
Male	4,597	54	32.9	68	8,600
Female	3,881	46	15.2	31	4,600
Race					
White	7,941	94	46.5	97	6,900
Black	426	5	1.1	2	3,600
Other	110	1	0.4	1	4,000
Age of recipient in May 1988					
16–24	161	2	0.1	0	800
25–34	2,348	28	6.0	12	2,900
35–44	3,149	37	14.7	31	5,500
45–54	1,666	20	12.2	25	9,200
55–59	545	6	7.7	16	18,900
60 or over	608	7	7.4	15	15,600

Age of recipient when most recent LS was received				
16–24	1,225	15	2.3	5	2,100
25–34	3,755	45	13.3	28	4,100
35–44	2,042	25	15.2	32	8,500
45–54	850	10	10.1	21	14,500
55–59	214	3	4.7	10	26,800
60 or over	171	2	2.0	4	15,400
1988 earnings of recipient				
$1–$4,999	345	5	3.0	8	10,500
$5,000–$9,999	616	9	1.8	5	3,300
$10,000–$14,999	954	13	3.0	8	3,600
$15,000–$19,999	1,113	15	4.7	13	5,100
$20,000–$24,999	1,045	14	4.6	13	5,000
$25,000–$29,999	818	11	4.6	13	6,400
$30,000–$49,999	1,761	24	8.8	25	6,200
$50,000 or more	561	8	4.9	14	10,300

Table 5.4 (continued)

SOURCE: Piacentini (1990b).

NOTES: Tabulations by the Employee Benefit Research Institute of the May 1988 Current Population Survey Employee Benefit Supplement.

a. Aggregate and average amounts may be understated. While 8.5 million workers are estimated to have received LSs as of May 1988, data on the amount of the most recent LS received are available for just 7.1 million of these individuals. Therefore, the aggregate amount of most recent LSs received excludes the LSs received by the remaining 1.4 million workers, leading to an understatement of aggregate amounts received. However, if no systematic relationship exists between the amount of LS received and whether or not the amount is reported, distributions and averages will not be affected. (Without evidence of the nature of such a relationship, the effect on estimated averages is ambiguous.) In addition, in the May 1988 CPS EBS public use database, all LSs reported to be greater than $99,999 in nominal dollars have been topcoded at $99,999. An estimated 36,800 workers had received LSs equal to or in excess of this amount as of May 1988. Therefore, both aggregate and average amounts may be understated to the degree that the amounts received by these workers actually exceeded this amount.

b. Individual items may not add to total because some respondents did not report some characteristics of recipients or lump sum distributions.

c. Bases of percentages exclude respondents for whom recipient and lump sum distribution characteristics were not reported.

d. Rounded to nearest $100.

e. Because the survey was conducted in May 1988, includes only LSs received in the first four or five months of 1988.

Table 5.5
Distribution of Lump Sum Recipients by Demographic Characteristics
of Recipients, 1983 and 1988

Worker characteristics	1983 %	1988 %	Change
Sex			
Male	55	54	-1
Female	46	46	0
Age			
Under 25	3	2	-1
25 – 34	33	28	-5
35 – 44	32	37	5
45 – 54	19	20	1
55 or over	13	13	0
Income			
$1–$4,999	8	5	-3
$5,000–$9,999	13	9	-4
$10,000–$14,999	17	13	-4
$15,000–$19,999	16	15	-1
$20,000–$29,999	22	25	3
$30,000–$49,999	13	24	11
$50,000 or more	5	8	3

SOURCE; Atkins (1986); Piacentini (1990b).
NOTE: Individual items may not add to total due to rounding. Bases of percentages exclude
respondents for whom recipient and lump sum characteristics were not reported.

Table 5.6
Distribution of Preretirement Lump Sum (LS) Recipients by Amount of Lump Sum Received, by Selected Economic and Demographic Characteristics, 1988

Worker characteristics	Total receiving LS distributions (thousands)[a]	Amount of most recent LS distribution (constant 1988 dollars)					
		Not reported (%)	$1-$999 (%)	$1,000-$4,999 (%)	$5,000-$9,999 (%)	$10,000-$19,999 (%)	$20,000 or more (%)
Total	8,478	6	24	34	13	8	6
Sex							
Male	4,597	16	19	33	14	9	9
Female	3,881	16	29	34	13	6	3
Race							
White	7,941	16	23	34	14	8	6
Black	426	13	25	33	9	5	15
Other	110	9	42	32	1	10	6
Age in May 1988							
16-34	2,509	10	41	38	6	4	2
35-44	2,042	18	15	29	16	12	9
45-54	850	20	13	28	18	8	13
55 or over	385	23	6	23	13	13	23

Age when most recent LS was received							
16-24	1,225	18	38	37	6	[b]	1
25-34	3,775	20	24	34	12	7	2
35-44	2,042	18	15	29	16	12	9
45-54	850	20	13	28	18	8	13
55 or over	385	23	6	23	13	13	23
Year in which most recent LS was received							
1988[c]	451	10	28	41	7	8	6
1987	1,220	10	33	31	11	9	6
1986	920	10	30	29	14	9	8
1980-1984	2,403	14	24	35	13	9	6
1975-1979	1,191	18	20	38	13	4	6
1970-1974	579	19	17	38	14	5	7
Before 1970	624	28	8	35	16	9	4
1988 earnings							
$1-$9,999	1,577	48	17	19	11	2	3
$10,000-$14,999	954	14	33	35	11	4	3
$15,000-$19,999	1,113	16	29	34	11	7	3
$20,000-$24,999	1,045	13	28	32	15	10	2
$25,000-$29,999	818	12	20	42	11	11	4

Table 5.6 (continued)

Worker characteristics	Total receiving LS (thousands)[a]	Amount of most recent LS (constant 1988 dollars)					
		Not reported (%)	$1-$999 (%)	$1,000-$4,999 (%)	$5,000-$9,999 (%)	$10,000-$19,999 (%)	$20,000 or more (%)
30,000-$49,999	1,761	20	20	34	14	7	5
$50,000 or more	561	15	13	35	12	11	13
Not reported	1,265	19	17	28	13	9	13
May 1988 pension status[d]							
Nonparticipant	2,672	16	24	33	14	8	5
Participant	4,500	16	23	34	13	8	6
Defined benefit[e]	2,370	18	22	34	14	8	4
Defined contribution[e]	1,022	11	28	39	11	5	6
Not reported	1,108	19	20	31	11	10	10

SOURCE: Piacentini (1990b).

NOTE: Tabulations by the Employee Benefit Research Institute of the May 1988 Current Population Survey Employee Benefit Supplement.

a. Individual items may not add to total because some respondents did not report some information.

b. Less than 0.5 percent.

c. Because the survey was conducted in May 1988, includes only LSDs received in the first four to five months of 1988.

d. A worker is considered to be a pension participant if he or she reported inclusion in a pension, retirement, profit sharing, stock, or 401(k)-type plan at a wage and salary job, or reported a self-employed job and contributions to an IRA or Keogh.

e. A large degree of response error may be present in worker responses on plan type.

Recipient choices for lump sum distributions in 1988 can be divided among savings and consumption categories. Of the 13 percent of recipients who reported rolling at least part of a distribution into tax-qualified savings, 11 percent invested in IRAs and 2 percent invested in a deferred annuity or other retirement plan (table 5.7). When the broadest definition of savings is used, including all financial savings, buying a house, paying a mortgage, and paying loans or debts, 65 percent of recipients reported some savings. Forty percent of recipients reported consuming part of a distribution. They defined that consumption as car purchase, education expense, unemployment expenses, and "other" uses.

The 1983 data show that young recipients more commonly consume some of their distribution, and the 1988 data indicate this also. Half of those age 16 to 24 reported some consumption, while 4 percent reported some tax-qualified savings (table 5.7). Consumption drops to 39 percent in the next two age categories (25-34 years and 35-44 years) and to 29 percent in the age 55 and over category. Figures for tax-qualified savings show the opposite pattern, rising steadily over the age categories to 36 percent in the age 55 and over category.

There is a marked increase in use of tax-qualified financial savings over the years in which the most recent lump sums were received. Almost 25 percent of recipients reporting a lump sum in 1988 used some for tax-qualified savings and 74 percent reported using some portion for savings as broadly defined (table 5.7). This compares to 15 and 66 percent in 1980-84 and 2 and 61 percent in 1970-74.

Use of tax-qualified savings drops from 13 to 11 percent when use of the total lump sum distribution rather than a part is examined, and under this condition the broadest definition of savings drops from 65 to 59 percent (table 5.8). Thirty-four percent of recipients report consuming the entire lump sum distribution. These 34 percent represent only 21 percent of total distributions (table 5.9). The much smaller group who reported using only tax qualified vehicles for lump sums, 11 percent, account for 22 percent of the total amount of the money distributed in lump sums.

The determinants of using a preretirement lump sum for savings in 1988 differ from those found in 1983 data. Andrews (1990b) used 1988 data to determine that when retirement savings are narrowly defined as savings placed in an IRA, a deferred annuity, or in another retirement

Table 5.7
Proportion of Lump Sum (LS) Recipients Reporting Various Uses for Any of Their Most Recent Lump Sum Distribution, 1988

Worker characteristics	Received LS from prior job (thousands)[a]	Proportion of recipients using any of their LS					
		IRA (%)	Insurance annuity or retirement plan (%)	Tax-qualified financial savings[b] (%)	Financial savings[c] (%)	Savings[d] (%)	Consumption[e] (%)
Total	8,478	11	2	13	35	65	40
Sex							
Male	4,597	12	3	15	36	67	38
Female	3,881	10	2	11	34	62	41
Race							
White	7,941	11	2	14	36	65	40
Black	426	6	f	6	24	59	42
Other	110	17	f	17	26	76	24
Amount of most recent LS							
$1-$499	1,042	3	g	3	21	50	50
$500-$999	955	6	1	6	31	62	40
$1,000-$2,499	1,627	8	1	8	28	62	43
$2,500-$4,999	1,220	16	1	17	38	68	37
$5,000-$9,999	1,114	17	4	21	44	74	33
$10,000-$19,999	660	23	5	28	54	80	33
$20,000 or more	495	22	10	29	57	81	30

Age when most recent LS was received							
16-24	1,225	3	1	4	24	51	50
25-34	3,755	9	2	10	32	67	39
35-44	2,042	13	2	15	38	66	39
45-54	850	22	5	26	50	70	35
55 or over	385	31	7	36	61	75	29
Year in which most recent LS was received							
1988[h]	451	18	5	23	46	74	31
1987	1,220	18	3	20	46	72	37
1986	920	15	3	18	39	70	38
1985	800	15	2	17	45	72	30
1980-1984	2,403	13	3	15	36	66	38
1975-1979	1,191	6	1	7	22	57	46
1970-1974	579	1	1	2	25	61	40
Before 1970	694	f	1	1	24	47	55
1988 earnings							
$1-$9,999	961	6	1	7	32	63	45
$10,000-$14,999	954	6	2	8	24	56	46
$15,000-$19,999	1,113	11	1	12	31	68	37
$20,000-$24,999	1,045	11	1	12	35	62	44
$25,000-$29,999	818	10	2	11	35	66	39

Table 5.7 (continued)

Worker characteristics	Received LS from prior job (thousands)[a]	IRA (%)	Insurance annuity or retirement plan (%)	Tax-qualified financial savings[b] (%)	Financial savings[c] (%)	Savings[d] (%)	Consumption[e] (%)
					Proportion of recipients using any of their LS		
$30,000-$49,999	1,761	14	3	16	38	63	40
$50,000 or more	561	20	6	25	55	78	30
May 1988 pension status[i]							
Nonparticipants	3,977	10	2	12	34	65	40
Participants	4,500	12	3	15	36	65	39

SOURCE: Data from Piacentini (1990b).
NOTE: Tabulations by the Employee Benefit Research Institute of the May 1988 Current Population Survey Employee Benefit Supplement.
a. Individual items may not add to total because some respondents did not report some information.
b. Includes IRAs, insurance annuities, and other retirement programs.
c. Includes tax qualified savings accounts, and other financial instruments.
d. Includes all financial savings, purchase of a house, payment of a mortgage, and payment of loans or debts.
e. Includes purchase of a car, education expenses, expenses incurred during a period of unemployment, and other uses.
f. No observations in category.
g. Less than 0.5 percent.
h. Because the survey was conducted in May 1988, includes only LSs received in the first four to five months of 1988.
i. A worker is considered to be a pension participant if he or she reported inclusion in a pension, retirement, profit sharing, stock or 401(k)-type plan at a wage and salary job, or reported a self-employed job and contributions to an IRA or Keogh.

Table 5.8
Proportion of Lump Sum Recipients Reporting Various Uses for All
of Their Most Recent Lump Sum Distribution by Demographic Characteristics, 1988

Worker characteristics	Received LS from prior job (thousands)[b]	Tax-qualified financial savings[c] (%)	Financial savings[d] (%)	Proportion of recipients using all of their lump sum distribution[a]		Mixed consumption and savings (%)
				Savings[e] (%)	Consumption[f] (%)	
Total	8,478	11	30	59	34	5
Sex						
Male	4,597	12	30	61	32	6
Female	3,881	10	30	57	36	5
Race						
White	7,941	11	31	59	34	5
Black	426	4	21	52	36	7
Other	110	9	24	76	24	g
Amount of most recent LS						
$1-$499	1,042	3	21	50	49	1
$500-$999	955	6	28	59	37	3
$1,000-$2,499	1,627	7	24	56	38	5
$2,500-$4,999	1,220	14	33	62	31	5
$5,000-$9,999	1,114	18	36	67	25	7
$10,000-$19,999	660	23	42	67	20	13
$20,000 or more	495	22	44	70	19	12

Table 5.8 (continued)

Proportion of Lump Sum Recipients Reporting Various Uses for All of Their Most Recent Lump Sum Distribution by Demographic Characteristics, 1988

Worker characteristics	Received LS from prior job (thousands)[b]	Proportion of recipients using all of their lump sum distribution[a]				
		Tax-qualified financial savings[c] (%)	Financial savings[d] (%)	Savings[e] (%)	Consumption[f] (%)	Mixed consumption and savings (%)
Age when most recent LS was received						
16-24	1,225	4	23	49	47	2
25-34	3,755	9	28	61	33	6
35-44	2,042	13	30	60	33	6
45-54	850	20	41	62	27	8
55 or over	385	28	53	70	23	6
Year in which most recent LS was received						
1988[h]	451	21	43	69	26	5
1987	1,220	16	39	61	27	11
1986	920	15	32	61	30	9
1985	800	15	39	69	27	3
1980-1984	2,403	13	30	60	33	5
1975-1979	1,191	5	19	53	42	4
1970-1974	579	1	21	59	38	2
Before 1970	694	1	21	44	52	3

1988 earnings					
$1-$9,999	961	6	28	54	36	9
$10,000-$14,999	954	5	19	52	42	4
$15,000-$19,999	1,113	11	26	62	32	5
$20,000-$24,999	1,045	10	31	56	38	6
$25,000-$29,999	818	9	30	60	34	5
$30,000-$49,999	1,761	14	34	59	36	4
$50,000 or more	561	22	45	69	21	9
May 1988 pension status[i]					
Nonparticipants	3,978	10	28	58	51	6
Participants	4,500	12	32	60	27	5

SOURCE: Data from Piacentini (1990b).

NOTE: Tabulations by the Employee Benefit Research Institute of the May 1988 Current Population Survey Employee Benefit Supplement.

a. For purposes of determining exclusive uses of LSs, "don't know" and missing responses were taken as "no" responses. For example, a worker whose only "yes" response was to the IRA option was classified here as using his or her entire LS for "tax-qualified savings" even if the worker's response to one or more nontax-qualified options was "don't know" or missing. Some workers did not respond "yes" to any of these options; therefore, mutually exclusive horizontal percentages may add to less than 100 percent.

b. Individual items may not add to total because some respondents did not report some characteristics.

c. Includes IRAs, insurance annuities, and other retirement programs.

d. Includes tax-qualified savings, savings accounts, and other financial instruments.

e. Includes all financial savings, purchase of a house, payment of a mortgage, and payment of loans or debts.

f. Includes purchase of a car, education expenses, expenses incurred during a period of unemployment, and other uses.

g. Less than 0.5 percent.

h. Because the survey was conducted in May 1988, includes only LSs received in the first four to five months of 1988.

i. A worker is considered to be a pension participant if he or she reported inclusion in a pension, retirement, profit sharing, stock, or 401(k)-type plan at a wage and salary job, or reported a self-employed job and contributions to an IRA or Keogh.

Table 5.9

Proportion of Aggregate Amount of Lump Sum (LS) Distributions Used Entirely for Selected Purposes, 1988

Worker characteristic[b]	Received LS from prior job (billions)[c]	Proportion of aggregate LS amounts reportedly used entirely for:[a]					
		Tax-qualified financial savings[d] (%)	Financial savings[e] (%)	Savings[f] (%)	Consumption[g] (%)	Mixed consumption and savings (%)
Total	48.1	22	44	70	21	9
Sex						
Male	32.9	19	44	71	19	11
Female	15.1	29	46	68	26	6
Race						
White	46.5	22	45	70	21	9
Black	1.1	4	18	49	31	15
Other	0.4	34	57	69	30	[h]
Amount of most recent LS						
$1-$499	0.3	3	19	48	50	1
$500-$999	0.7	7	28	57	39	3
$1,000-$2,499	2.7	7	23	57	38	5
$2,500-$4,999	4.4	15	34	63	31	5
$5,000-$9,999	7.9	17	35	68	24	8
$10,000-$19,999	8.9	25	43	68	19	13
$20,000 or more	23.2	26	53	75	16	9
Not reported	12.7	24	49	76	16	7

Age when most recent LS was received						
16-24	2.3	6	17	38	57	3
25-34	13.3	13	28	65	26	9
35-44	15.2	20	41	67	24	9
45-54	10.1	25	55	78	7	15
55 or over	6.8	41	75	82	14	3
Year in which most recent LS was received						
1988[i]	2.5	36	59	71	26	3
1987	6.3	23	49	65	18	16
1986	5.8	26	36	58	23	19
1985	5.1	14	61	78	15	7
1980-1984	13.8	23	45	74	18	8
1975-1979	7.5	26	39	75	21	4
1970-1974	3.4	14	47	78	17	5
Before 1970	3.2	[h]	14	44	49	5
1988 earnings						
$1-$9,999	4.8	25	58	74	17	9
$10,000-$14,999	3.0	10	25	56	32	11
$15,000-$19,999	4.7	24	41	77	18	5
$20,000-$24,999	4.6	21	34	63	28	9
$25,000-$29,999	4.6	11	28	56	33	11
$30,000-$49,999	8.8	27	54	72	22	5
$50,000 or more	4.9	21	42	65	13	21

Table 5.9 (continued)
Proportion of Aggregate Amount of Lump Sum (LS) Distributions Used Entirely for Selected Purposes, 1988

Worker characteristic[b]	Received LS from prior job (billions)[c]	Proportion of aggregate LS amounts reportedly used entirely for:[a]				
		Tax-qualified financial savings[d] (%)	Financial savings[e] (%)	Savings[f] (%)	Consumption[g] (%)	Mixed consumption and savings (%)
May 1988 pension status[j]						
Nonparticipants	21.5	21	41	70	20	9
Participants	26.6	22	47	69	22	9

SOURCE: Data from Piacentini (1990b).

NOTE: Tabulations by the Employee Benefit Research Institute of the May 1988 Current Population Survey Employee Benefit Supplement.

a. Aggregate amounts are understated by an unknown amount. While 8.5 million workers are estimated to have received LSs as of May 1988, data on the amount of the most recent LS received are available for just 7.1 million of these individuals; therefore, the aggregate amount of most recent LSs received excludes the LSs received by the remaining 1.4 million workers. In addition, in the May 1988 CPS EBS public use database, all LSs reported to be greater than $99,999 in nominal dollars have been topcoded at $99,999. An estimated 36,800 workers had received LSs equal to or in excess of this amount as of May 1988; therefore, aggregate amounts are understated to the degree that the amounts received by these workers actually exceeded this amount.

b. For purposes of determining exclusive uses of LSs, "don't know" and missing responses were taken as "no" responses. For example, a worker whose only "yes" response was to the IRA option was classified here as using his or her entire LS for "tax-qualified savings" even if the worker's response to one or more nontax-qualified options was "don't know" or missing. Some workers did not respond "yes" to any of these options; therefore, mutually exclusive horizontal percentages may add to less than 100 percent.

c. Individual items may not add to total because some respondents did not report some characteristics.

d. Includes IRAs, insurance annuities, and other retirement programs.

e. Includes tax-qualified savings, savings accounts, and other financial instruments.

f.Includes all financial savings, purchase of a house, payment of a mortgage, and payment of loans or debts.

g.Includes purchase of a car, education expenses, expenses incurred during a period of unemployment, and other uses.

h. Less than 0.5 percent.

i. Because the survey was conducted in May 1988, includes only LSs received in the first four to five months of 1988.

j. A worker is considered to be a pension participant if he or she reported inclusion in a pension, retirement, profit sharing, stock, or 401(k)-type plan at a wage and salary job, or reported a self-employed job and contributions to an IRA or Keogh.

Table 5.10
Use of Lump Sum Distributions Before and After Major IRA Legislation, 1960-1988

Year received	Recipients	Number rolling entire distribution	Percentage rolling entire distribution	Estimated 90 percent confidence interval[a]
		(weighted estimates)		
1988[b]	450,590	93,758	20.81	7.02
1987	1,219,609	199,021	16.32	3.88
1986	919,929	136,160	14.80	4.30
1985	800,486	117,964	14.74	4.60
1984	474,866	69,612	14.66	5.96
1983	485,851	62,152	12.79	5.56
1982	493,629	64,465	13.06	5.57
1981	484,848	51,774	10.68	5.15
1980	463,352	59,826	12.91	5.72
1975-1979	1,191,413	62,069	5.21	2.36
1970-1974	579,015	5,077	0.88	1.42
1960-1969	558,033	7,149	1.28	1.75
Before 1960	135,805	507	0.37	1.92
Don't know	185,928	11,588	6.23	6.51
Missing	34,275	0	0.00	0.00
Total	8,477,629	941,122	11.10	1.25

Table 5.10 (continued)

Year received	Recipients	Number rolling entire distribution	Percentage rolling entire distribution	Estimated 90 percent confidence interval[a]
		(weighted estimates)		
Groupings and differences				
Tax reform				
1987-1988	1,670,199	292,779	17.53	3.41
1982-1986	3,174,761	450,353	14.19	2.27
Difference			3.34	4.10
IRA deduction expansion and IRA marketing				
1982-1986	3,174,761	450,353	14.19	2.27
1975-1979	1,191,413	62,069	5.21	2.36
Difference			8.98	3.28
ERISA and inception of IRAs				
1975-1979	1,191,413	62,069	5.21	2.36
Before 1975	1,272,853	12,733	1.00	1.02
Difference			4.21	2.58

SOURCE: Unpublished Employee Benefit Research Institute tabulations prepared by Joseph S. Piacentini for the U.S. Department of Labor.
a. Based on formula provided by the U.S. Bureau of the Census as part of CPS documentation.
b. Part-year data—survey conducted in May 1988.

Table 5.11
Calculation of Estimated Value of Preretirement Lump Sum
Distributions Not Placed in Retirement Savings, 1990
(Dollars in millions)

Pension payments—administrative data, 1987	
Trusteed defined benefit payments paid to participants (Form 5500)	$44,935
Insurance payments (not including individual policies)	$16,390
Total pension payments	$61,325
Pension payments survey data, 1987	
December 1989 Current Population Survey	
Retirees (private and self-empoyed)	$36,386
Spouses of retirees (private estimate)	$5,724
Total pension payments	$42,110
Ratio of administrative to survey data (estimate of undercount)	1.456
Preretirement distributions survey data, 1987	
December 1989 Current Population Survey	
Workers age 40-54—private sector	$2,823
Nonworkers age 40-54—private sector	$127
All individuals age 40-54	$2,950
May 1988 Current Population Survey	
Workers under age 40—private sector	$1,854
All preretirement distributions	$4,805
Preretirement distributions, 1987	
Adjusted for undercount	$6,998
Preretirement distributions, 1990	
Rough adjustment to 1988 CPI	$7,638
Rough adjustment to 1989 DC assets	$8,393
Distributions not rolled over, 1990	
Based on CPI adjustment	$5,958
Based on DC asset adjustment	$6,547

SOURCE: Fu Associates, *Lump-Sum Distributions: A Comparison of Administrative and Survey Data.* Arlington, VA: 1990.

program, workers most likely to have invested lump sum distributions in this way were older, were more recent recipients of a distribution, were owners of an IRA in 1988, received dividends in 1988, and were homeowners. The 1983 data found relatively high rates of savings for retirement, using a similarly narrow definition, only among those who received large lump sums and were either older or were college educated (Atkins 1986).

Analysis of 1988 data found that recipients increasingly used tax-qualified savings vehicles. Those who contributed to a current IRA more commonly used a lump sum for retirement savings than for current spending. Since 1975, the use of IRAs as a repository for distributions has steadily increased. Table 5.10 shows the use of rollovers to IRAs by lump sum recipients pre- and post-major legislation. Following the imposition in 1987 of a 10 percent excise tax on lump sum distributions that were not rolled over into another tax-qualified retirement vehicle, the percentage of recipients making rollovers increased, but the increase was not sufficiently large to be statistically significant. Based on patterns in prior years, plans paid an estimated $6.0 to $6.5 billion in 1990 preretirement distributions that job leavers did not put into IRAs, annuities, or employer plans (Table 5.11).

CONCLUSIONS

Preretirement lump sum distributions became increasingly available during the decade of the 1980s and the number of pension plan participants who exercised the option to receive a lump sum at job change is substantial, particularly among younger workers.

A large share of those who took a lump sum distribution did not roll it over into a tax-qualified vehicle or other retirement plan. However, the percentage of recipients using some part of a preretirement lump sum distribution for tax-qualified savings increased during the 1980s.

NOTE

1. This chapter was written by Phyllis Fernandez.

6

Pensions and Layoffs

Quits are the focal point for most studies investigating the effects of job change on pension benefit losses and the opposing effects of pension benefit losses on job change.[1] Quits and layoffs are behaviorally distinct, and portability policies designed to address quit-related issues may fail to address important issues related to layoffs. Moreover, unless layoffs are explicitly considered, portability policies could have an undesirable impact on workers who lose their jobs or on firms who must lay off workers to remain economically viable. This chapter provides information on the magnitude of layoffs in the U.S. economy and discusses the relative importance of quits versus layoffs. It also examines possible effects of layoffs on portability losses.

LAYOFFS IN THE U.S. ECONOMY

Employers may find it necessary to dismiss their employees, either because of poor economic conditions or because of poor performance by the employee or the company. These dismissals can be temporary or permanent. In a temporary layoff, a worker may be off the job for weeks or months, but is eventually reemployed by the company that initiated the layoff. A worker who is permanently laid off must either find a new job or drop out of the labor force. Because temporary layoffs are not relevant to pension portability issues, this chapter is concerned with permanent layoffs only.

Permanent layoffs sometimes result from deficient demand for the company's product.[2] Deficient demand can arise for two reasons. First, it can result from structural changes in the economy, brought about by competition from imports or loss of international competitiveness by U.S. firms, automation and other types of technological change, changing consumption patterns, or loss of regional competitiveness. Deficient demand can also occur as part of the business cycle.[3] Both structural and cyclical layoffs and layoffs associated with a company's poor performance manifest themselves through plant closings, plant relocations, shift or position phaseouts, or closure of the entire business. Layoffs resulting from poor performance by the worker show up as individual dismissals.

Before the mid-1980s, information on the number of permanent layoffs was sketchy, and estimates ranged widely. However, in January 1984, the Bureau of Labor Statistics added a special supplement on displaced workers to the Current Population Survey. This supplement, which is referred to as the first Displaced Worker Survey (DWS), and two additional supplements added in January 1986 and January 1988 are the primary sources for most of the information on the extent of permanent layoffs in the U.S. economy.[4]

As shown in table 6.1, estimates from the first Displaced Worker Survey indicate that 13.9 million workers 20 years of age and older lost their jobs between January 1979 and January 1984 because of plant closings, employers going out of business, or layoffs from which they had not been recalled (Flaim and Sehgal 1985). Eliminating the 2.4 million workers who lost their jobs for seasonal reasons, or for other reasons that could not be classified, leaves an estimated 11.5 million workers who were permanently laid off during this period.[5] The second survey, which examined layoffs between January 1981 and January 1986, estimates slightly fewer layoffs—approximately 10.8 million over the five-year period (Horvath 1987). This represents approximately 2.2 million workers per year, as opposed to 2.3 million for the 1979-84 period.

The number of layoffs varies over the business cycle, with more layoffs occurring during economic downturns and fewer layoffs occurring during upswings. Because the periods covered by both the first and second surveys included severe recessions, layoff estimates of 2.2 and 2.3 million workers per year are probably at the high end of the range when averaging over a business cycle. The third Displaced Worker Survey was conducted during an economic upswing; it examined layoffs between January 1983 and January 1988. Unfortunately, the information published from this survey does not include an estimate of the total number of permanent layoffs; instead, it presents information on the number of permanent layoffs among workers with three or more years of tenure. By comparing this information with similar information from the first two surveys, it is estimated that during this period 2.0 million workers per year were permanently laid off.[6] Combining this estimate with the estimates from the two previous surveys suggests that during the decade of the 1980s an average of 2.0 to 2.3 million workers were permanently laid off from their jobs each year.

Table 6.1
Layoff Statistics, 1979-1988
(in millions of workers)

	First DWS	Second DWS	Third DWS
Number of workers losing jobs	13.9	NA	NA
Number of workers permanently laid off	11.5	10.8	NA
–with 1 or more years of tenure	7.1	6.8	NA
–with 2 or more years of tenure	6.9	NA	NA
–with 3 or more years of tenure	5.1	5.1	4.6
–with 5 or more years of tenure	3.2	NA	NA

SOURCES: Flaim and Sehgal (1985); U.S. Department of Labor (1985); Horvath (1987); Herz (1990).
NOTE: The first Displaced Worker Survey (DWS) covers the period between January 1979 and January 1984; the second DWS covers January 1981 through January 1986; and the third DWS covers January 1983 through January 1988.

In general, there are more quits than layoffs in U.S. labor markets.[7] However, the quit rate, like the layoff rate, varies over the business cycle—except that quits are higher when the economy is booming and lower when the economy is in recession. As a result, there may be some years when layoffs exceed quits. Data from the *Employment and Training Report of the President* (1982, table C-13) show that although the (temporary and permanent) layoff rate was considerably higher than the quit rate throughout the first half of the 1960s, this was the case in only three years (1975, 1980, and 1981) between 1965 and 1981.

The situation appears to be similar for pension plan participants; in general, for these workers the number of quits exceeds the number of layoffs. Using panel data for males age 31-50 from the 1983-86 Survey of Consumer Finances (SCF) and the 1984-87 Panel Study of Income

Dynamics (PSID), Gustman and Steinmeier (1990) show that 60 percent of the males who had a pension on their initial job and who changed jobs reported that they changed jobs voluntarily. The statistics are similar to the rates for job changers who did not have a pension. According to the SCF, 59 percent of the job change by those without a pension on their initial job were voluntary; in the PSID, the figure was 64 percent.[8]

LAYOFFS AND LOSS OF PENSION BENEFITS

As is the case with quits, layoffs can result in pension benefit losses. This section first attempts to identify the number of workers who are at risk of pension benefit loss. This is followed by a discussion of the types of benefit losses that may be incurred by workers who are laid off.

Pension Coverage of Laid-off Workers

Evidence on the number, or percentage, of laid-off workers who are covered by a pension is sketchy. Unfortunately, none of the three Displaced Worker Surveys includes any questions about pensions, so they cannot be used to determine pension coverage among laid-off workers. Instead it is necessary to turn to other sources.

These sources suggest that a smaller portion of laid-off workers are covered by pension plans than is the case for workers as a whole.[9] Gustman and Steinmeier (1990) present descriptive statistics indicating that 40.7 percent of the involuntary movers in their sample from the 1984-87 PSID were covered by a pension on their lost job, whereas 60.6 percent of their entire sample was covered. Calculations based on descriptive statistics from the Survey of Income and Program Participation (SIPP) and the SCF make a similar point (Gustman and Steinmeier 1990, tables 1, A1, and A4). In the SIPP, 39.6 percent of the involuntary movers had a pension in their initial job, while this figure was 63.7 percent for the sample as a whole. The SCF figures were 63.6 percent and 74.8 percent.[10] All three samples consisted of males who were 31-50 years old at the beginning of the sample period.

In an earlier study using the National Longitudinal Survey of Mature Men, Parnes and King (1977, p. 83) found that about half of their sample of displaced workers were covered by pensions, versus three-quarters of nondisplaced workers. They examined male wage and salary workers over age 45 who had been with their employer for over five years and who were permanently separated from the employer between 1966 and 1971.

It is tempting to conclude from this evidence that between 40 and 60 percent of the 2.0 to 2.3 million workers who were permanently laid off each year during the 1980s were covered by a pension. However, because the samples cover males only, this is not correct. Females have a lower probability of being laid off than their male counterparts, and this results in an overrepresentation of males among displaced workers.[11] Despite this problem, the information can be used, along with other data, to arrive at a rough estimate.

Estimates of the number of displaced workers (from the Displaced Worker Survey) include both male and female full-time and part-time workers. According to data from the Current Population Survey (CPS) pension supplement, the pension coverage rate for full-time and part-time workers was 42 to 43 percent during the 1980s (Beller and Lawrence 1992).[12] Assuming that the ratio between the percentage of laid-off workers covered by a pension and the percentage of all workers covered by a pension is roughly the same in the CPS data as it is in Gustman and Steinmeier's PSID data, and assuming that the distribution of full-time versus part-time workers in the CPS supplement on displaced workers is the same as it is in the CPS pension supplement, it is estimated that during the 1980s slightly less than 30 percent of the 2.0 to 2.3 million laid-off workers were covered by a pension. This implies that between one-half and two-thirds of a million workers lose all or some of their pension benefits each year due to layoffs.[13]

Pension Losses Associated with Vesting Requirements

Laid-off workers who are unvested lose their rights to future retirement benefits. Although estimates of the number of unvested laid-off workers are not available, some information can be gleaned from the tenure statistics for displaced workers. Current regulations require vesting after five years for most workers.[14] According to the first Displaced Worker Survey, approximately 28 percent of the 11.5 million workers who were permanently laid off between January 1979 and January 1984 had five or more years of tenure (table 6.1).[15] This suggests that about 70 percent of the 550,000 to 600,000 pension-covered workers who lose their jobs each year also lose their pensions because they have not vested.

This estimate is certainly too high. For pension participants as a whole, only 23 percent of all private-sector full-time pension plan participants are not vested (Piacentini 1990b).[16] Because displaced workers generally have less tenure than the population as a whole (Blau and Kahn 1981; Madden 1988), it is reasonable that a larger percentage of displaced workers will not be vested. However, a 50 percent differential is not realistic.

Part of the differential can be attributed to the fact that the data from the Displaced Worker Survey are not strictly comparable to those for all pension participants. In particular, the DWS statistics include part-time workers, which inflates the estimate of the percentage of workers who are not vested. Another part of the differential is due to the fact that a small number of pension plans offer full and immediate vesting, so that at least some of the displaced workers with fewer than five years of tenure will be vested. A third factor in the differential is that the pension participant statistics are for workers with partial as well as full vesting, whereas the Displaced Worker Survey tenure statistics are proxies for the full vesting standards. Finally, the major part of the differential is probably due to tenure statistics being a poor proxy for vesting statistics.

The data for pension participants suggest that this is the case. Based on these data, 54 percent of all private-sector full-time workers have fewer than five years of tenure (Piacentini 1990b, table 1). However, data from the same source indicate that only 23 percent of all private-sector full-time pension plan participants are not vested. The most likely explanation for this discrepancy is that workers who participate in pension plans tend to have more years on the job than workers who do not participate. If this is true for displaced workers—and there is no reason to suggest it is not—then considerably less than 70 percent of the 550,000 to 600,000 pension-covered workers who lose their job each year are unvested.

Pension Losses Associated with Backloading

As is the case for workers who quit, a laid-off worker who is fully vested in a defined benefit plan will suffer a pension benefit loss even if he/she is able to immediately find a new job offering the same compensation package as the old job. This is because in a defined benefit plan benefits are frequently tied to wages near retirement. A worker who is laid off before retirement will receive benefits based on his/her wage before the layoff. Because these benefits are generally not adjusted to take into account inflation occurring between the layoff and the time at which the employee would have been eligible to retire, the worker will suffer a benefit loss.

Displaced workers who are covered by defined contribution plans will generally not incur losses due to backloading. Thus whether this type of benefit loss is an important policy issue for displaced workers depends in part on how many of these workers are covered by defined benefit plans. In the workplace as a whole, about 68 percent of all workers in pension plans participate in a defined benefit plan (Beller and Lawrence 1992, p. 6). However, this percentage may not be as high for displaced workers. Dorsey (1987) finds a positive relationship between permanent layoffs and the primary pension plan being a defined contribution plan. Using industry layoff rates, he finds that a one standard deviation increase in the permanent layoff rate (.20 per 100 workers) raises the likelihood of defined contribution coverage by about 2 percent. When the probability of permanent layoffs is high, companies may tend to offer defined contribution plans rather than defined benefit plans. This could occur, for example, if the company recognizes that it is susceptible to intense foreign or domestic competition, automation, or changing consumption patterns. In this way, employees will not suffer a loss from backloading if they are laid off.[17]

Pension Losses Associated with Lump Sum Distributions

A third major source of pension portability loss stems from preretirement lump sum distributions. It is likely that the percentage of laid-off workers who receive lump sum distributions is higher than for the workforce as a whole. Although laid-off workers frequently receive unemployment insurance, severance benefits, trade adjustment assistance, and so forth, some may need additional money to carry them through a lengthy period of unemployment. For this reason, a higher percentage of laid-off workers may elect to receive a lump sum distribution and use all or part of it for current consumption.

A low percentage of workers receiving lump sum distributions use them for expenses incurred during unemployment (Piacentini 1990b). Only 11 percent of lump-sum recipients use any of their distribution for nondiscretionary consumption (educational expenses and expenses incurred during a period of unemployment), and only 8 percent use all of the distribution for this purpose.[18] However, even though a small percentage of lump-sum recipients use their distribution to carry them through a period of unemployment, the distribution could be quite important for that minority.

CONCLUSIONS

At least half a million pension-covered workers are laid off each year. While some of them suffer large pension losses, as well as a loss in earnings, two factors mitigate the loss for many workers. First, workers who are laid off tend to have relatively short job tenure. Second, workers who are laid off are more likely to have a primary defined contribution plan than are other pension covered workers.

NOTES

1. This chapter was written by Tabitha Doescher.

2. Some permanent layoffs manifest themselves as opportunistic behavior on the part of the firm. For example, a firm may promise pensions to some of its workers and then lay off some workers so that it does not have to meet its pension obligations. The firm could be engaging in deceptive behavior (which would be illegal) or it could be responding to unexpected changes in its situation (e.g., changes brought about by deficient demand).

3. Many of the layoffs associated with a cyclical downswing will be temporary rather than permanent. However, some cyclical layoffs become permanent layoffs. This would be the case for example, when a cyclical decline lasts for several years.

4. All respondents to the January 1984, 1986, and 1988 CPS were asked if they or a member of their household age 20 or older had lost or left a job in the previous five years because of a plant closing, an employer going out of business, a layoff from which the individual was not recalled, or other similar reasons. An affirmative response led to additional questions about the reason for the job loss, the nature of the lost job (e.g., when it was lost, years of tenure, and earnings), and the individual's unemployment and reemployment experience. The three data bases

compiled from these Displaced Worker Surveys thus contain a wealth of information about layoffs during the 1980s.

5. This estimate does not (in concept) include workers who were discharged for cause. As a result, data from the DWS slightly underestimate the number of permanent layoffs. Using a small sample from the National Longitudinal Survey of mature men, Parnes and King (1977) found that 7.1 percent of the layoffs which occurred between 1966 and 1971 were discharges. The underestimate from the DWS is probably not that large since some discharged workers may rationalize that they were laid off because of slack work rather than fired for cause and may therefore be included in the survey. Another possible source of underestimation is the recall bias which may occur when an individual is asked to recall a past event. Some respondents apparently forget layoffs that occurred several years ago.

6. This estimate was obtained by (1) using both the first and second DWS to calculate the number of displaced workers with three or more years of tenure as a percentage of the number of workers who were permanently laid off (regardless of tenure), (2) taking the average of this percentage across both surveys and applying it to the number of displaced workers from the third DWS with three or more years of tenure to estimate total permanent layoffs over the five years covered by the third survey, and (3) dividing the estimate of total permanent layoffs by five to obtain an estimate of average annual layoffs. Data from the third DWS are from Herz (1990).

7. The distinction between quits and layoffs can be fuzzy. Some workers may quit their jobs in anticipation of being laid off or fired, while others may be laid off or fired immediately before the time they would have quit on their own.

8. Gustman and Steinmeier also examine panel data for males age 31 - 50 from the 1984-87 Survey of Income and Program Participation (SIPP), and these data tell a different story. First, in the SIPP data the number of quits is less than the number of layoffs among pension plan participants: only 43 percent of the SIPP job changers changed jobs voluntarily. Second, the SIPP data suggest that the incidence of involuntary turnover is considerably higher for job changers with pensions than for those without pensions: approximately 59 percent of the SIPP job changers who were without a pension on their initial job changed jobs voluntarily. In all likelihood, the reason for the discrepancy between the SIPP statistics and the SCF and PSID statistics rests with problems classifying job changes as quits or layoffs. In the SIPP data, of a total of 107 job changes, only 37 could be classified as either voluntary or involuntary. For this reason, the SCF and PSID data are probably more reliable for analyzing voluntary and involuntary turnover among job changers than the SIPP data.

9. One explanation for this is that jobs with a high probability of layoffs are less likely to offer pensions. Another possibility is that workers who are laid off have different characteristics than workers in general, and these characteristics are associated with low pension coverage. The evidence on this second possibility is unclear. For example, a disproportionate number of laid-off workers are from the manufacturing industry, which typically has a high rate of pension coverage. Estimates from the DWS suggest that about 40 to 50 percent of displaced workers were in jobs in manufacturing (Flaim and Sehgal 1985; Horvath 1987; Herz 1990). In addition, a disproportionate number of laid-off workers are male (about 64 percent in each of the three DWS), and males tend to have higher pension coverage rates. On the other hand, there is some speculation that small companies tend to have higher plant closing rates than large companies (Howland and Peterson 1988, p. 49); however, the pension coverage rate is lower at small firms than at large firms (Even and Macpherson 1990).

10. The reason for the difference in magnitude between the SCF statistics and the PSID and SIPP statistics is not clear, but may have something to do with small sample sizes and problems with the data (discussed in Gustman and Steinmeier 1990a and 1990b).

11. Both Blau and Kahn (1981) and Maxwell and D'Amico (1986) find that women have a lower probability of being laid off. Each of the Displaced Worker Surveys shows that approximately two out of three displaced workers were men (Flaim and Sehgal 1985; Horvath 1987; Herz 1990).

12. Covered workers includes those who have met a plan's eligibility requirements and are participating in the plan. It does not include workers who are employed with firms sponsoring a plan but who are not enrolled because they (a) do not meet age and/or service requirements, (b) are in an employee group excluded from the plan, or (c) chose not to participate.

13. This number should be used with caution. The estimate is based on the assumptions mentioned in the text, and it is not known whether these assumptions are valid. In addition, the reader should keep in mind that layoffs vary over the business cycle.

14. More specifically, the Tax Reform Act of 1986 sets out the following minimum vesting requirements: for plans with cliff vesting, it requires 100 percent vesting after five years (ten years for multiemployer plans); for plans with graduated vesting, it requires 100 percent vesting after seven years (20 percent after three years and 20 percent additional in each of the next four years). See Graham (1988) for a more complete discussion.

15. For these workers, the minimum vesting requirements were those specified by ERISA: 100 percent vesting after 10 years for plans with cliff vesting; 100 percent vesting after 15 years for plans with graduated vesting; the "rule of 45" for plans with alternative graded vesting; and a provision that each class must vest after five years for plans with class-year vesting. Since the purpose of this section is to get a ballpark estimate of the number of laid-off workers who might be expected to lose their pension rights under current regulations (rather than to estimate what actually happened to these particular workers), the current standard of five years of tenure is used.

16. Using the employee benefits supplement of the May 1988 CPS, Piacentini (1990b, Table 3) reports that 37 percent of all private-sector full-time workers are at least partially vested on their current job. Since 48 percent of all private-sector full-time workers are currently participating in a pension plan (Piacentini 1990b, Table 1), this suggests that 77 percent of all private-sector full-time pension plan participants are vested. This implies that 23 percent are not vested.

17. Dorsey suggests an alternate explanation. He views the rate of permanent layoff as a proxy for firm-financed specific training, with a high layoff rate indicating a low level of specific training. Companies in which workers have low levels of specific training have less incentive to attempt to tie workers to the firm and thus exhibit a higher incidence of defined contribution plans.

18. Note that these statistics will vary over the business cycle.

7

Pension Portability
in the United States

The U.S. pension system provides workers some portability through vesting, multiemployer plans, reciprocity, and portability networks. Although some portability arrangements currently benefit few workers, they are a logical starting point for discussing portability policy because they demonstrate options that could be extended to more workers.

PORTABILITY OF BENEFITS

An unvested job leaver loses all rights to a pension.[1] Prior to the passage of ERISA in 1974, some plans required workers to stay until retirement to vest. Dan McGill (1972) wrote, "The most sensitive (pension) issue of the moment is whether a pension plan should be required by law to provide for vesting *prior to retirement*" (p. 322, italics from the original). For full-time workers in 1972, only 53 percent of men and 39 percent of women covered by a private pension plan who had worked 20 to 24 years for one employer were vested (table 7.1).

Many plans before ERISA required a sum of age and service for vesting, 40 being the norm (McGill 1972, p. 11). A break in service before vesting canceled all accumulated benefit credits, and they were usually not restored if the worker returned to the firm. Some plans made former employees forfeit benefits if they worked for a competitor. Discouraging employees from working for competitors helped preserve the firm's trade secrets and protected it from competing against workers it had trained. Some firms also denied benefits to any employee guilty of misconduct. This action punished workers and secured restitution.

Table 7.1
Vesting Status of Private Pension-Covered Workers, 1972

Length of employment (in years)	Percentage distribution by vested status				
	Total	Vested	Not vested	Don't know	No response
Total					
Total[a]	100	32	51	15	1
Less than 5	100	20	60	20	1
5-9	100	25	59	16	1
10-14	100	36	49	15	1
15-19	100	47	41	11	1
20-24	100	50	38	12	b
25 or more	100	51	37	10	3
Men					
Total[a]	100	34	50	15	1
Less than 5	100	21	59	19	1
5-9	100	25	58	16	1
10-14	100	36	48	14	1
15-19	100	49	39	10	1
20-24	100	53	36	11	b
25 or more	100	52	37	9	2
Women					
Total[a]	100	26	55	18	1
Less than 5	100	16	61	22	1
5-9	100	24	60	15	1
10-14	100	34	50	15	b
15-19	100	39	47	14	c
20-24	100	39	46	13	2
25 or more	100	47	32	14	6

SOURCES: Bureau of the Census; Kolodrubetz and Landay (1973).
a. Vested status totals include workers not responding to length of employment on current job, not shown separately.
b. Less than 0.5 percent.
c. Not calculated where base is less than 200,000.

The passage of ERISA improved worker status by offering benefit protection through vesting requirements. Once vested, an employee cannot become divested. Plans may use any vesting method with a waiting period not exceeding ERISA standards. Two common methods are cliff vesting and graded vesting.

Under cliff vesting, in which a worker jumps from zero to full vesting after working a specified period of time, ERISA initially required workers to fully vest within 10 years. Large defined benefit plans typically used this schedule. In a nationally representative survey taken prior to enactment of the Tax Reform Act of 1986, 90 percent of plans using cliff vesting had a 10-year waiting period (U.S. General Accounting Office 1990).

Under graded vesting, in which the percentage of vested benefits periodically rises until the worker is fully vested, ERISA's standard (initially) required that, at a minimum, a worker be partially vested after five years, and his/her vesting rights rise a fixed percentage yearly until reaching full vesting after 15 years. Small defined contribution plans used this schedule.

Disability, death, or early retirement benefits generally do not vest if they are more generous than the actuarial equivalent to normal retirement benefits. To receive these benefits, the employee must be working for the employer when the contingency occurs.

The Tax Reform Act of 1986 shortened vesting for single-employer pension plans. It cut the maximum years a worker must wait for full vesting from 10 to 5 for cliff vesting. For graded vesting, it cut the 5-to-15-year period to 3 to 7 years, with 20 percent vesting after 3 years. The Tax Reform Act lowered the minimum age for vesting credit from 22 to 18 years old.

Multiemployer plans, to which several employers contribute under collective bargaining agreements, satisfy the Tax Reform Act's requirements if participants fully vest after 10 years. Participants in these plans earn credit for service with any employer funding the plan. Multiemployer lobbyists argue that longer vesting schedules are appropriate for their plans because participants still earn service towards vesting after switching jobs. As a result, job leavers vest in situations where vesting would not occur in a single-employer plan.

The U.S. General Accounting Office (1990) studied the accelerated vesting required by the Tax Reform Act. Under the old rules, many participants in cliff plans did not work long enough to become vested, but would be fully vested under the new rules. The GAO figured that 9 of 10 plans of large employers had to cut the years required for vesting to comply with the Tax Reform Act. By contrast, half the plans of small employers had to change vesting rules. The Employee Benefit Research Institute estimated the added cost of five-year cliff vesting at 2 to 7 percent of private pension plan contributions to the system as a whole (Employee Benefit Research Institute 1986a).

ERISA demands more stringent vesting standards in some cases. Accrued benefits deriving from the worker's contributions must vest immediately. Worker contributions and salary reduction contributions to a qualified cash or deferred arrangement—a 401(k) plan—as well as the investment earnings from those contributions, also must be fully vested and nonforfeitable at all times. Similarly, contributions to a Simplified Employee Pension (SEP) must vest immediately. SEPs were authorized through the Revenue Act of 1978 to enable smaller employers to start pensions without the complexity and administrative expense of a traditional pension plan.

Faster vesting standards, set by the Tax Equity and Fiscal Responsibility Act of 1982 (TEFRA), are also required for "top- heavy" plans. A top-heavy plan, by definition, provides most of the benefits to key workers, including the company's owners, officers, and highly compensated workers. One of two vesting standards must be met. The first requires the worker to fully vest after three years. The second standard is six-year graded vesting, in which the worker must be at least 20 percent vested after two years, with this percentage rising over four more years, until 100 percent vesting is reached after six years.

Congress enacted TEFRA legislation to ensure that plans of smaller employers provided broadly based coverage for all workers, not just for those with an ownership or management position. In 1987, 57 percent of defined benefit plans were top-heavy. However, 84 percent of top-heavy plans had less than 10 participants (Turner and Beller 1992).

PORTABILITY OF SERVICE

Portability of service is the transfer of service credit between plans of different employers when a worker changes jobs. It is predominantly an issue for defined benefit plans. It is usually not an issue for defined contribution plans because employer contributions are based only on current salary, with service not affecting the amount the employer or employee contributes to the plan. In some defined contribution plans, however, the employer contributes a larger share of salary for workers with long tenure.

Multiemployer Plans

Multiemployer pension plans, which are predominantly defined benefit plans, provide portability of service. They are collectively bargained plans covering workers in an industry or craft within a fixed geographic area. They enable workers to change jobs without losing service credit when they resume work with another employer in the plan.

Multiemployer plans typically develop in industries with certain features. First, the industry has many small firms within a single geographic labor market. Second, the industry has high turnover of firms. Third, the industry has high worker turnover. Fourth, the industry is skilled-labor-intensive. Multiemployer plans are common in construction, trucking, the merchant marine and coal mining. Of the 3,066 multiemployer plans in 1988, 35 percent were defined contribution plans (Turner and Beller 1992, p. 590).

The decline in unionism has reduced the importance of multiemployer plans. The share of private pension participants in multiemployer plans fell from 19.8 to 14.8 percent from 1975 to 1988 (Turner and Beller 1992, p. 592).

Reciprocity

Service-credit transfer arrangements among plans are known as reciprocity agreements. Under these contracts, several plans, usually multiemployer plans covering members of local unions with the same international union, agree to give pension credit for service under any of the plans. With reciprocity, "two, or more, financially independent pension plans will each recognize employee service credited in the other participating plan, or plans, for the purposes of (1) establishing an employee's eligibility to accrue benefit credits, (2) determining an employee's entitlement to receive benefits from a plan, and/or (3) determining the benefits payable to an employee" (McDonald 1975). Reciprocity may be between plans of unrelated employers, related employers, or the same employer.

Reciprocity agreements are common among multiemployer plans. In multiemployer arrangements, the plan rather than a particular employer ultimately pays the benefits. Between 45 and 50 percent of multiemployer plans have reciprocity with another plan (Meier and Bassett 1981). These agreements are concentrated in motor transportation, clothing, construction, and water transportation industries.

Reciprocity is uncommon among single-employer plans. The only study on portability and reciprocity agreements among single-employer plans, using 1975 data, found that only 8 percent of single-employer plans had reciprocity with unrelated employers (Grubbs 1981). Reciprocity agreements are more common among very large plans. For plans with 1,000 or more participants, 20 percent of defined benefit plans and 19 percent of defined contribution plans had reciprocity agreements.

The prevalence of reciprocity arrangements varies greatly by industry and union status. For plans overall, 8 percent of both collectively bargained and noncollectively bargained plans had reciprocal arrangements. In the finance, insurance, and real estate industry sector, 54 percent of collectively bargained plans and 4 percent of noncollectively bargained plans had portability or reciprocity arrangements with plans of other employers. In manufacturing, however, the figures dropped to 7 percent and 10 percent, respectively.

Reciprocity agreements take two forms.[2] Under the "money follows the worker" approach, a pension member working temporarily in another jurisdiction has the pension contribution that jurisdiction requires sent to his/her "home" plan. The employee receives pension credits for the contributions according to the rules of the home plan. The second form of reciprocity agreement is the *"pro rata"* approach, where a pension participant accruing credits under several plans will receive a pension benefit from each. The sum due from each is figured as though combined service applied to that plan, and it is then prorated according to service in that plan. Under this approach money is not transferred between plans. Reciprocity preserves benefits by broadening the definition of continuing service. It is thus similar to break-in-service rules, allowing workers to return to an employer and count service before and after the break.

Portability Networks

A portability network, or clearinghouse, holds pension funds and combined benefits from various plans. There are 11 centrally administered networks or clearinghouses of unrelated employers, all but two of which have been operating since 1963.

Each of these networks covers a single industry's workers and permits service portability for workers transferring between employers in the network. The largest network is the Teachers Insurance and Annuity Association and the related College Retirement Equities Fund (TIAA-CREF). Some others are the National Automobile Dealers Association, the National Health and Welfare Mutual Life Insurance Association, the National Education Association, and the Savings Banks Retirement System.

The networks have various arrangements to transfer vested credits between employers. AT&T provides a good example. The divestiture of AT&T on January 1, 1984, prompted the formation of a new portability network, resulting in the division of two pension plans—covering one million workers—into eight plans (Schmitt 1988). The new plans for each regional holding company accepted the service credits for reassigned workers or those who otherwise moved between or among AT&T and the divested companies and former Bell System workers who returned to work with AT&T. Service credit for figuring benefit eligibility and amounts is recognized as if there were a single company.

Grubbs (1981) studied 25 portability networks, including networks among related employers. The networks were classified into two groups. The first consisted of the 10 centrally administered portability clearinghouses existing at the time covering employers not under common control. The second, comprised of other portability networks and plans with portability aspects, consisted of pension plans of a single employer or an employer group under common control, and some plans offering portability to any other pension plan.

Grubbs obtained data on nine of the ten centrally administered networks, the oldest of which began in 1918. Some networks, such as the

National Automobile Dealers Association, were started by employer associations formed for other purposes. Others, like TIAA-CREF, formed to meet retirement needs of employers and workers in an industry, but are not affiliated with an employer association having other functions. Some networks have only a single plan or a single plan type; others sponsor various plans. Individual employers choose to participate in one or more types. Together, the nine networks covered 2 percent of active U.S. pension participants.

Because each network is limited to a single industry, workers often move among participating employers. If a social worker employed by one employer in the National Health and Welfare network ends employment, his/her next employer in all probability will be a participating employer in that network.

The nine networks are nonprofit, but with differing forms of organization. The TIAA-CREF and National Health and Welfare plans are organized as life insurance companies. Others are organized as trusts, with management by the trust or a related company. The portability they provide varies. Service with any participating employer is often treated as service with the current employer in figuring worker eligibility to participate in, vest in, or receive benefits from the plan. If a worker is entitled to benefits based on employment with several employers, most networks combine the benefits into a single check.

The clearinghouses allocate benefit liabilities differently. For defined contribution plans, each employer's cost for benefits is the sum of the contributions allocated to its workers. For defined benefit plans, actuaries figure costs for each employer as though a separate plan were maintained for that firm. Or, they figure costs for the network, or some segment of it, and an allocation is made to individual employers, perhaps as an equal share of pay for all employers with the same benefit formula. Even if the network calculates costs separately for each employer, the service of all retired workers is usually combined. This is done by purchasing annuities at retirement or by using a similar uninsured approach.

All nine networks handle most of the administrative work for the plans, thus minimizing the administrative work for individual employers. The networks often maintain direct communication with individual participants. Four networks provided data showing that from 2 to 15 percent of retiring participants receive benefits from employment with multiple employers.

Case Studies of Portability Networks

The National Automobile Dealers and Associates Retirement Trust (NADART) serves retail automobile dealerships belonging to the National Automobile Dealers Association (NADA). If a worker transfers between employers with NADART money purchase or profit sharing plans and the new employer agrees, the worker's vested account balance is transferred to the new employer's plan. If a worker transfers between defined benefit plans, service in one plan counts towards vesting in the other.

The Teachers Insurance and Annuity Association (TIAA) incorporated as a legal reserve life insurance company in 1918. The College Retirement Equities Fund (CREF), founded in 1952, is a companion organization. CREF provides variable annuities with values depending on the common stocks in which the premiums are invested. All participating employers are nonprofit colleges, universities, independent schools, and related nonprofit research and educational institutions. In 1981, 80 percent of four-year colleges and universities provided TIAA-CREF coverage. Of the 3,200 participating institutions, 450 were publicly supported colleges and universities. The TIAA-CREF system uses fully portable individual annuity contracts. These contracts are vested in and owned by individual workers from the date they are issued.

The Savings Banks Retirement System provides benefits for employees of mutual savings banks. This system consists of 120 employers in seven states. Portability differs among the employers. In most plans, the service earned by a worker under a prior plan in the system counts towards eligibility for early retirement, disability retirement, and preretirement spouse's benefits. Nineteen plans recognize prior service with a former system employer for figuring benefits. The benefit based on total service is offset by any benefit available from the prior plan. In effect, this results in the current employer raising the benefit accrued with prior employers.

Controlled Groups

Portability is also available within a controlled group, which is defined as a group of firms with 80 percent or more common ownership.[3] While pension law does not require service portability among unrelated employers, it does require some service portability among related employers, which includes firms under common control, trades or businesses (whether or not incorporated) under common control, and some affiliated service groups.

ERISA requires that work for all employers in a controlled group be counted as work for a single employer in calculating a worker's eligibility to participate and, later, to vest in a plan. Thus, the service of a worker transferring to a related employer must be used in figuring whether the worker is vested under the new employer's plan, but it need not be used in calculating a worker's benefit. As a business practice, some employers count all service with controlled group members when determining benefit levels.

If a firm is sold to a new owner, federal law also requires an employer maintaining a plan of a predecessor employer to treat service for the predecessor as service for the current employer.

Large Firms

The extent of portability can be measured by the relationship between the plans having such arrangements. The most extensive situation is portability applying to unrelated employers. Less extensive is portability applying to plans of related (controlled group) employers. Least extensive is portability applying only to the same employer's plans. If a job change within a large firm requires the worker to change pension plans, the plans generally are set up so that the worker loses no future pension benefits.

PORTABILITY OF ASSETS

Preretirement Distributions

Portability of assets is the transfer of a worker's pension assets from one plan to another when he/she changes jobs. Defined contribution plans often give the worker a lump sum of money when he/she leaves the firm. The cashout is the worker's account value.

Present law allows portability of assets by permitting them to be rolled over, or transferred, from one tax-favored retirement arrangement to another. It also induces workers to save money received from pension plans for retirement. Vested workers enrolled in defined contribution plans do not lose benefits unless they opt to receive a lump sum. If they leave their money in the plan, the account accumulates investment earnings as if the workers had not changed jobs.

Transfers from Plans

Funds generally cannot be distributed to a worker from a pension plan before the end of employment, but contributions to profit-sharing and stock bonus plans are distributable within two years of the contribution, even if the job has not ended. Some employers prefer not to offer lump sum distributions from defined benefit plans because doing so reduces the plan's funding ratio for underfunded plans.

Many plans cash out benefits of under $3,500 because the employer wants to avoid the administrative burden of managing small accounts for former employees. If the worker's present value of benefits exceeds $3,500, the benefit cannot be distributed before the earliest of normal retirement age or 62, unless the worker consents to the distribution. Workers with benefits with present values of more than $3,500 may opt to leave the benefits in the plan until retirement age, thus preserving the benefits until retirement.

Tax Treatment of Preretirement Distributions

The Tax Reform Act of 1986 encourages workers to save preretirement lump sum distributions. It imposes a 10 percent tax if lump sum distributions are not rolled over into an IRA or an employer-sponsored plan within 60 days of receipt. Because the tax is an income tax, it applies to the part of a lump sum includable in income. In 1992 the further requirement of 20 percent withholding was added on distributions not rolled over within 60 days.

The tax does not apply to the following distributions: (1) those received after age 59 1/2; (2) those received due to the individual's death; (3) those received due to the individual's disability; (4) those used to pay medical expenses that would be deductible if the individual itemized deductions (not applicable to IRAs);[4] (5) those paid as equal periodic payments over the life expectancy of the individual (or the joint life expectancies of the individual and spouse); (6) those made for a worker separating from service after age 55 (not applicable to IRAs); (7) those received from an employee stock ownership plan; or (8) those made under a qualified domestic relations order in a divorce settlement (not applicable to IRAs).

The Tax Reform Act further induces workers not to take preretirement distributions. Under prior law, an individual receiving a lump sum distribution could apply 10-year income averaging to the distribution. The Act phased out 10-year forward averaging, allowing workers instead a one-time five-year forward average for a lump sum distribution after the worker reaches age 59-1/2. Also, under prior law, that portion of a distribution attributable to contributions before January 1, 1974, could qualify as a long-term capital gain. The Act phased out the use of long- term capital gains treatment over six years.

The Tax Reform Act also changed rules on the treatment of tax basis when an individual receives a distribution from a tax-favored retirement arrangement to which he/she and the employer have contributed. If the worker received a sum before the date the plan began paying the worker an annuity, prior law treated the worker as first receiving non-taxable income and then receiving taxable income. The Act modified the basis recovery rules for pre-annuity starting date distributions to provide for the pro-rata recovery of basis. Thus, a worker is entitled to exclude from taxation a portion of the payment figured by multiplying the payment by the ratio of his/her basis to the accrued benefit under the plan. In making this change, Congress decided the prior rule permitted the accelerated tax-free recovery of worker contributions and thus encouraged the nonretirement use of tax-favored retirement arrangements.

Rollovers

A rollover is a tax-free transfer of pension assets from one plan to another. A worker receiving a lump sum distribution from an employer-sponsored retirement plan may transfer it, less any after-tax employee contributions, to an IRA where it can still receive tax-deferred investment income.[9] The tax code also permits the funds to be transferred into another employer's plan, but few plans accept such rollovers. Partial rollovers of lump sum distributions into an IRA are permitted if at least half the worker's account balance is rolled over.

A rollover into an IRA is a substitute strategy for making a portability transfer to another employer's plan. A distribution rolled over into an IRA is excluded from income and is not subject to the 10 percent excise tax on early distributions. When such sums are later distributed from the IRA, they are includable in income. A total distribution may be rolled over to an IRA if made due to the individual's death; after the individual has reached age 59 1/2; due to ending employment (other than for a self-employed person); or for self-employed persons only, if the person becomes permanently disabled. Only employer contributions (and income on employer or worker contributions) may be rolled over into an IRA. Distributions of worker contributions cannot be rolled over.[5]

Distributions from qualified retirement plans are rolled over into another qualified plan on the same basis that distributions are rolled over into an IRA. Law does not require plans to permit transfers or rollovers from another qualified plan. Plans permitting such transactions are most common among related employers or with a merger or acquisition.

Grubbs (1981) surveyed plans to investigate the acceptance of rollovers by pension plans. He found that 93 percent of plans did not accept rollovers. Of the plans accepting rollovers, 96 percent placed the rollovers in individual accounts and 4 percent did not specify how the rollover would be treated. Two percent of defined benefit plans with fewer than 100 participants and 1 percent of plans with 100 or more participants accepted rollovers. Nine percent of defined contribution plans with fewer than 100 participants and 5 percent with 100 or more participants accepted rollovers.

SOCIAL SECURITY

Social security provides the majority of retirement income for most workers. In 1988 only 2 percent of elderly households received at least

50 percent of income from private pensions, while 55 percent received at least 50 percent from social security (Turner and Beller 1992). Most workers are now covered by social security, and benefit accruals are portable among all employers included in the system. Social security portability is possible because plan design, funding, and administration are done centrally, by Congress and the Social Security Administration. Social security benefits are based on lifetime earnings, so a worker changing jobs loses no benefits under this plan. Expanding social security would solve portability problems. Projections show, however, that the rising old-age dependency ratio will reduce social security benefits relative to earnings (Doescher and Turner 1988).

NOTES

1. The discussion in this section draws heavily from U.S. General Accounting Office (1990).

2. The following discussion of reciprocity is taken from Brownlee (1989).

3. Material in this section is taken largely from Joint Committee on Taxation (1988).

4. The tax does not apply to lump sum distributions that are used to pay medical expenses that are deductible for federal income tax purposes (that is, in excess of 7.5 percent of adjusted gross income).

5. Employee contributions are treated differently because such contributions (other than to 401(k) plans) are taxable.

8

Pension Reform Debate

Inevitably, raising pension benefits or reducing risks involves costly changes, and there are winners and losers. Reformers must identify the market imperfection that suggests the need for government intervention and analyze the arguments for pension reform, which fall into five overlapping categories: (1) equity, (2) tax and budget policy, (3) government regulation, (4) economic effects, and (5) financial responsibility.

Rather than analyzing the arguments, this chapter debates them—first presenting the strongest argument in favor of pension reform and then the strongest argument against it. On the final issue of financial responsibility, the debate is not pro or con but who should pay—employers, government, or workers.

EQUITY

Equity arguments are motivated by value judgments about fair treatment of similar and dissimilar groups. Opinions differ as to what defines an equitable balance between costs and benefits for competing groups. Workers, firms, and taxpayers compete for lower taxes, higher tax subsidies, lower costs, and higher and more secure benefits. In the case of pension reform, at least one group bears costs when another benefits.

Short-Tenure versus Long-Tenure Workers

Pension portability raises the benefits of short-tenure workers. In a fixed-benefits budget, this advantage comes at the expense of other workers.

Pro

A full pension should not depend on 30 years of tenure with one employer. With incomplete pension portability, job leavers receive reduced benefits for the years they have worked. Because women in pensions plans have shorter job tenure than men, pay via pensions favors men at women's expense. Tax-favored pensions should not be an employer monopoly. Short-tenure workers and job leavers cannot compensate for their disadvantage in pension plans by maintaining comparable tax-favored savings because the only comparable form of savings, IRAs, has low contribution limits. Workers should be free to receive a tax-favored pension without tying themselves to one employer.

Con

Employers value long-tenure workers and should be able to reward them through generous pensions. While pension portability raises the benefits of short-tenure workers, those workers may have preferred higher wages. When this is the case, short-tenure workers view themselves as worse off with pension portability. The frequency with which job leavers take lump sum distributions supports this point.

Workers versus Firms

Equity issues between workers and firms depend on who owns the pension assets. Are they owned by workers, firms, or both? Whose interests should the plan favor? Pension law requires plans to invest assets solely in the interest of participants. It does not require, however, that all elements of pensions favor workers at the firm's expense. Elements of plan design that allow inflation to erode retirement benefits if taken before retirement are precisely those elements employers depend on to encourage loyalty and long service.

Pro

Workers want the reduced risk of benefit loss that government regulations provide, and portability reduces the risk that workers will lose benefits due to job change. Employers favor pension regulations with which they already comply. These regulations may cut the risk of benefit loss perceived by workers even though the plan is already complying with the regulation. Some employers favor pension reforms forcing competitors to bear the same benefit costs they do.

Con

Favoring long-service workers is a good compensation strategy for many employers. Workers and firms both gain from long-term commitments from workers to firms.

TAX AND BUDGET POLICY

The tax issue raised in pension reform deals with two important elements: who benefits from the tax expenditures, and how much does pension reform cost the Treasury Department in lost revenue.[1] In a period of large budget deficits, political reality   requires pension reform to refrain from adding to the budget deficit. This translates into a demand that pension reform be revenue neutral: it must be packaged so that higher tax expenditures for some aspects of pensions are offset elsewhere in the budget by higher tax revenues or lower tax expenditures.

Pro

It is wrong that pension tax advantages are enjoyed disproportionately by long-tenure workers, because the primary public purpose of pension plans is to provide retirement income, not to reward worker longevity.[2] Further, the longevity subsidy depends largely on inflation, which is beyond the control of employers or employees. Even if favoring longevity were desirable, subsidizing job tenure in an inflation-dependent way is a questionable undertaking given inflation rate variability.

Con

Congress uses the tax system for many social purposes, and there is no reason why worker longevity should not be included.

GOVERNMENT REGULATION

As budget deficits grow, the federal government looks increasingly at the option of mandating benefits. This intervention, however, raises the issue of government's role as regulator.

Pro

If it expands choices, government intervention through pension reform is desirable. The value of freedom of choice is raised by expanding the range of alternatives and giving workers more control over their pension arrangements. Because government subsidizes benefits, it has a right and duty to decide how that tax subsidy should be distributed and how job change should reduce tax benefits. It also has an obligation to set minimum standards to protect relatively powerless workers.

While a basic conflict of goals exists between maintaining a free market and protecting workers from economic risks, protecting workers, at least to a point, overrides philosophical concerns about an unfettered market. Moreover, government mandates are often not aimed at protecting the typical worker, but are motivated by social goals already achieved by many workers. Mandates aim at protecting vulnerable workers.

Workers, even if given options, do not always make the "right" choices. Paternalistic reformers identify "merit goods," and argue that these should be provided even if workers do not choose them. Paternalistic reformers argue that workers undersave for retirement due to an inability to plan for distant needs; thus, portability must be mandated to raise retirement savings.

Poor information exchange further justifies government intervention. Workers or firms who are poorly informed about the advantages and costs of a benefit arrangement may seek less than adequate benefit plans. For example, workers frequently underestimate their life expectancies and save too little for retirement. When information problems are difficult to correct, it may be necessary for government to require benefit coverage.

Externalities (costs to third parties) also justify government intervention. Because government provides public benefits to indigent retirees, retirees with low savings impose costs on society. Government may force workers to internalize the costs by requiring minimum retirement saving or may favor raising pension benefits to shrink social security's burden as the population ages. Finally, economies of scale argue for government intervention. Government could operate a portability clearinghouse more efficiently than the private sector, given the economies of large operations.

Con

Government intervention through pension reform coerces firms and workers and distorts market outcomes, allocating resources suboptimally. The labor market decides the optimal level and mix of benefits. It does so based on differing values placed on nonwage compensation by firms, workers, and labor unions.

Pension reform restricts choices by interfering when management and labor negotiate salaries. Requiring uniform minimum treatment of covered workers, pension reform restricts employer freedom to negotiate packages that meet worker needs. It arbitrarily assigns higher priority to one benefit at the expense of others. Pension reform may restrict worker consumption by prohibiting preretirement lump sum distributions. Worker well-being declines when workers prefer cash wages over the extra benefits that reform forces them to accept.

The expanded choices that result from government intervention cause adverse selection. This occurs because workers with longer than actuarial life expectancy choose a benefit available on better terms considering their own knowledge of life expectancy. The more choices there are, the more room there is for adverse selection. Such behavior raises the cost to employers of pension benefits.

Mandating portability disrupts pension plan administration. Any mandated change requires new plan practices, and plans must hire attorneys and employee-benefit specialists to assure compliance. To achieve a goal over the range of possible situations, government regulations often become highly complex, eventually making simplification itself a goal of reform. Mandates often require government to provide services and enforce new regulations, thus increasing the federal bureaucracy. Lacking a profit motive, government is less efficient than the private sector.

Underlying the paternalistic arguments for pension reform is the question of adequacy: do workers save adequately for retirement? Most undoubtedly do. The mandate of a paternalistic government diminishes incentive for responsible individual behavior and private charity. Further, and of most importance, mandates designed to raise benefits ultimately do the opposite. By raising costs, mandates frequently force firms to reduce or end benefits.[3]

ECONOMIC EFFECTS

Pension reform alters behavior of workers and firms, affecting job mobility and productivity. It also impacts retirement savings, affecting the type of pension plan firms provide and whether, in fact, they provide a plan. It may affect the ages and numbers of workers firms hire.

Job Mobility and Labor Market Efficiency

The loss of pension benefit with job change penalizes and reduces mobility. The economic efficiency of pensions affecting labor mobility varies between firms and over time, depending on economic conditions.

Pro

Some workers must change jobs to adjust to a dynamic economy. Changes in technology and imports, and growing and declining employment in different geographic areas and businesses, cause workers to change jobs. The United States, facing greater competition in the world economy, needs to foster job mobility. Higher workforce flexibility is essential for efficiency. The flexibility of the U.S. labor force would rise if pensions were linked to the worker rather than the job.

Con

The view that impediments to job change are undesirable supposes that worker productivity is highly transferable between jobs, and that any shift in relative prices or technology makes job change efficient. In contrast, labor economists stress causes and effects of long-duration jobs. The contract theories of long-duration jobs imply that reduced job mobility is efficient. Defined benefit pensions appear to have a productivity-augmenting role by discouraging quits, encouraging firms to invest in workers, and penalizing workers who "shirk."

Government portability mandates reduce efficiency by making it more difficult for firms to retain labor. Workers would be more likely to change jobs, and, consequently, employers might find it less advantageous to train workers. Portability also worsens labor-management relations by reducing worker loyalty to employers.

Unlike mandated social security participation, workers can choose whether or not to participate in the private pension system. That firms and workers agree on pension plans with quit penalties suggests that mobility would otherwise be excessive. Why would both voluntarily impede worker freedom to change jobs when an alternative—the defined contribution plan—offers tax advantages without penalizing separation?

Cost and International Competitiveness

Imports and exports are playing an increasingly large role in the U.S. economy, causing international competitiveness to be an increasingly important consideration in labor market decisions.

Pro

Portability increases labor market flexibility, raising U.S. international competitiveness. Portability may raise the cost of benefits, but the higher costs imposed on employers by pension reform are offset by lower cash wages than they would otherwise have to pay. Because such an offset occurs, the higher initial costs imposed on employers would not reduce their international competitiveness. In any case, exchange rates adjust and international trade is based on comparative advantage rather than absolute advantage.

Con

Pension reform makes domestic firms less competitive than foreign firms, raising employer costs, reducing U.S. competitiveness, and costing jobs. Higher costs cause firms to hire fewer workers or to favor some workers over others. If firms view women as short-tenure workers, and pension reform reduces the penalty on short-tenure work, a firm needing long-tenure workers for efficient operations would favor hiring men over women.

Defined Benefit versus Defined Contribution Plans

Will mandated pension portability raise employer costs and reduce pension coverage, especially by defined benefit plans? Are defined benefit plans better for workers than defined contribution plans? An answer of "no" to either question greatly simplifies the portability issue. Defined benefit plans could be required to provide greater portability. That would raise costs and reduce their advantages to employers, accelerating the shift from defined benefit to defined contribution plans. Or all pensions could be required to be defined contribution plans with benefits locked in until retirement.

Pro

For many portability proposals affecting defined benefit plans, converting a defined benefit plan to a defined contribution plan would be an attractive alternative to the employer. While defined benefit plans offer important advantages over defined contribution plans, problems triggered by mandating portability cause a shift from defined benefit to defined contribution plans. Employers have discovered the advantages of defined contribution plans: predictable costs, fairly easy administration, less government interference, and highly portable assets.

Con

Mandating portability raises pension costs, which results in firms opting out of pension coverage. While terminating a plan may seem drastic, defined benefit plan terminations were common in the 1980s and early 1990s. Thus, regulations intended to provide workers with a more secure pension instead trigger the end of the pension.

Many analysts have concluded that defined benefit plans provide more retirement income security than defined contribution plans. The employer is primarily responsible for the investment risk in defined benefit plans, while the worker bears the investment risk in defined contribution plans. Defined benefit plans are more widely used than defined contribution plans in nearly all countries, probably because firms are better able than workers to bear the investment risk. Also, most defined benefit plan benefits are guaranteed by the Pension Benefit Guaranty Corporation. Defined benefit plans benefit employers by affecting workforce age structure. Workers are encouraged to stay during prime productivity years, and are encouraged, by early retirement incentives, to quit when they grow older.

Old-Age Economic Security and National Savings

Private pensions play an important role in old age security and national savings. With the aging U.S. population and low U.S. savings rates, some analysts are concerned as to whether the private pension system is performing adequately.

Pro

Mandating portability raises pension benefits for some retirees, increasing old age security. Banning preretirement distributions has a similar effect. Such an approach could also raise national savings, by encouraging greater savings in pensions.

Con

The raised savings and benefit security would be undone if reform decreased the likelihood that firms would provide pensions, or caused them to provide less generous pensions. Also, workers frequently undo higher savings by reducing other forms of retirement assets. Thus, the positive effects on national savings and benefit security are likely to be minimal.

FINANCIAL RESPONSIBILITY

Regardless of how desirable portability reform is for equity, tax policy, government regulation, or economic effects, someone must pay for the higher benefits. Pension reform changes contractual relationships. Reforms effectively take financial assets from some people and give them to others. In the long run, the issue becomes, who pays?

Three parties may pay for pension reform: (1) employers (and ultimately consumers and stockholders), (2) government (taxpayers), (3) other workers covered by pensions and workers benefiting from pension reform. A complete analysis considers the minimizing strategies the paying party will entertain.

Employers

Many proposals designate employers as payers. The proposals do so, in part, because it seems unfair to make a job stayer pay for a job leaver's pension. If employers pay, the burden is borne by the firm the worker is leaving, the firm the worker is joining, or both. When employers pay, pension reform compels shareholders to surrender financial assets to mobile workers.

Actuaries and employee benefit consultants would intensely scrutinize pension portability reform to reduce employer cost and search for ways to redesign pension plans to provide satisfactory benefits at affordable prices. To compete in both labor and product markets, employers may redesign pension plans to keep costs at a previous level and shift costs by reducing pension generosity and/or by providing smaller cost-of-living increases for retirees.

Mandating that employers pay for pension reform does not resolve who ultimately pays. In addition to dropping a defined benefit plan or cutting its generosity, employers may try to shift the burden within the plan to the remaining workers and to retirees. Most employers, however, feel more responsibility for their retirees and current workers than for former workers.

Pension reform affects firms unequally. Because reform raises costs, established firms with a higher percentage of older workers bear a heavier burden.[4] It is thus misleading in analyzing pension reform to focus on average costs; one should consider the range of cost impacts on employers.

Government

Some argue that if inflation is the culprit in most portability loss, government should pay the cost. Perhaps this burden would make government more circumspect about inflationary policies. Due to the unpredictability of inflation, most employers are unwilling to take on the inherent liability. Whether that argument is accepted, mandating portability may cost government dearly in lost tax revenue. Any change in pension regulations that raises pension contributions, reduces lump sum cashouts, and raises pension assets, will decrease federal tax revenue.

Workers

The manner in which labor markets set wages and pension coverage is an important pension policy element. Economists base their views on the theory of equalizing differences, which holds that for costs paid by employers, workers, in turn, pay for pensions and pension reform through reduced cash wages and other benefits. The theory holds that employers in competitive markets offer equivalent compensation packages to similar workers. Thus, pension-covered workers must receive lower wages than similar workers without pensions.[5]

Because competitive forces set the value of compensation, employers tailor benefit packages to attract the workers they want. Employers wishing to attract long-term workers offer better pension benefits and lower current wages. Employers not needing long- tenure workers offer packages with greater immediate rewards. If the labor market operates as suggested by this theory, workers pay for pension reform by exchanging wages for future pension benefits. The total compensation they receive is unchanged. The theory does not imply that each worker exactly pays through reduced wages for the benefits he/she receives, but that as a group workers pay. While the theory is intellectually appealing, it has thus far proven too difficult to verify empirically.

NOTES

1. Tax expenditures are the forgone tax revenues that arise due to tax deductions and the preferential nontaxation of some forms of income. Tax expenditures are logically equivalent to other government expenditures in that both reduce the amount of money left to the Treasury for other expenditures.

2. See, for example, Ozanne and Lindeman (1987).

3. This discussion is based in part on Mitchell (1991).

4. This discussion is taken largely from Conklin (1991).

5. This offset may be reduced if pension coverage increases worker productivity.

9

Policy Options
for Pension Portability

Numerous options would reduce pension benefit losses of workers who leave jobs before retirement. A brief history will demonstrate the range of alternatives that U.S. policymakers have considered but not enacted. This is followed by an examination of various options

Public policymakers have studied pension portability since the mid-1960s. In 1965 the President's Committee on Corporate Pension Funds, formed by President Kennedy, proposed a central clearinghouse to receive pension benefit distributions for job leavers. The Social Security Administration was to administer the clearinghouse. In the early 1970s, several years before passage of ERISA, pension reformers introduced bills in Congress that included voluntary portability arrangements. Senator Jacob Javits of New York in 1974 proposed the formation of a central fund where job leavers could transfer pension assets.

In 1980 the President's Commission on Pension Policy issued a report recommending a Minimum Universal Pension System. Under this system, all workers would be covered by a minimum mandated employer pension with immediate vesting. A portability clearinghouse would handle job leavers' benefits.

In 1988 a Department of Labor advisory group issued a report including the following recommendations: require preretirement distributions to go to an IRA or another employer's plan; maintain or enhance disincentives for preretirement distributions; study whether plans should be required to accept rollovers from other plans; require employers to set up Simplified Employee Pensions (SEPs) upon employee request; and study options to expand pension coverage, including mandating pensions for all employers.[1]

EARLIER VESTING

Private pension portability would be improved by requiring shorter vesting. Such proposals aim at defined benefit plans, which generally vest more slowly than defined contribution plans. Vesting could be reduced to three-year cliff vesting or could occur immediately. Immediate vesting would reduce the benefits the average pension-covered worker loses by 4 percent (from 14.8 to 14.2 percent) (table 9.1).

Table 9.1
Portability Loss with Full and Immediate Vesting

Portability loss (%)	Percentage of covered workers	
	Current vesting requirements	Immediate vesting requirements
40 to 49	6.3	6.0
30 to 39	13.4	13.6
20 to 29	19.4	19.2
10 to 19	15.2	14.9
1 to 9	4.6	3.0
None	38.4	39.2
Gain	2.7	4.2
Total	100.0	100.0
Average loss for all workers	14.8	14.2
Average loss for workers with a loss	23.3	23.4

SOURCE: Hay/Huggins (1988).
NOTE: The portability loss is the percentage difference between the retirement benefit the worker would have received if all service had been covered by the retirement plan of the last employer and the benefit that the worker actually received. A worker who worked from at least age 30 to age 65 under one pension plan would not have a loss under this definition, since the maximum credited service for the plans in the model was 35 years. A worker who worked for 35 years under one plan and received a vested benefit from a second plan would show a "gain."

A typical pension plan in the late 1980s provided annual pension benefit accrual of $100 to $500 early in a career (Hay/Huggins 1988, p. iii). For most workers the lump sum value for four years of work ranges from $400 to $2,000; thus, typical losses for unvested workers in single-employer plans with five-year vesting are less than $2,000.

Workers who change jobs after a short tenure have small benefits because of the brevity of their tenure and because most of them are young, low-income workers.

If vesting requirements were tightened, employers would probably react by paying lump sums to terminating employees with short service. If these small lump sum distributions were not rolled over into an IRA or saved, they would be unavailable for retirement income, and the shorter vesting would not have reduced portability losses.

PRERETIREMENT INDEXING OF BENEFITS

Second only to benefit losses due to preretirement cashouts are portability losses that occur because deferred vested benefits of job leavers are unindexed. Pension benefits of workers who change jobs erode in real value because the wages used to calculate the benefit are unindexed for future wage growth or inflation. Had these workers remained with the original employer, their accrued benefits would have been indexed by their growing wages.

Two policies could greatly reduce this cause of portability loss. The first would be to require that vested benefits be adjusted for preretirement inflation if they are left in the plan, or require the plan to incorporate expected inflation to adjust the final salary for calculating a lump sum distribution. The second would be to require that defined benefit plans credit workers for service at prior jobs.

Price Indexing

One option for pension preservation would require employers to calculate benefits at job change, and then index them to maintain real value until retirement. This approach would amend the tax code to require that defined benefit plans take the salary base they use to calculate deferred annuities and adjust it for inflation occurring between job end and initial receipt of pension benefits. Workers in career-average and flat-dollar benefit plans, as well as those in final-pay plans, would be protected.

This option would determine the present value of benefits using a nominal (market) interest rate to discount future liabilities, and then index that value. A computational alternative yielding a similar result would discount future benefits with a real interest rate.[2] For example, with a real interest rate of say 2 percent, a higher present value of benefits results than if a nominal market interest rate were used. The plan then would maintain this benefit value unindexed. This option places the cost of portability reform, at least initially, on the employer who loses an employee. Revising defined benefit plans this way raises aggregate plan costs or redistributes benefits to short-service workers.

Under a second alternative, vested pension credits and an appropriate sum would be transferred to a pension clearinghouse or central pension bank. The clearinghouse would index benefits for preretirement inflation, and assess all participating employers an annual charge to cover the preceding year's cost of inflation. The clearinghouse must assess how much money should be transferred from a pension fund to the clearinghouse for a pension credit; and it must assess, allocate, and collect the annual cost of inflation, including possible charges or credits for bad or good investment returns. Any requirement should avoid price indexing that exceeds what former workers would have received had they stayed with the firm. The increase in the index could be limited to inflation or to average growth in wages for workers covered by the plan, whichever is smaller.

A related option would require that benefits of job leavers be indexed for preretirement inflation, but if inflation exceeds a cap, benefits would increase at the cap rate. Mandatory indexing could be set at the lesser of 5 percent or the Consumer Price Index. Other alternatives include indexation at the inflation rate minus a stated percent. In addition, indexing need not use a specific index, such as the Consumer Price Index, but could take the indirect form of adding years to a worker's service used for calculating benefits.[3]

Plans could still cash out small deferred annuities. Present value calculations, however, would discount the deferred annuity, using the real interest rate implied by the plan's actuarial assumptions (the nominal interest rate minus the inflation rate), rather than its nominal interest rate assumption. This change would be required to adjust for increases in nominal benefits needed to maintain the real value of benefits. Indexing could also be targeted to groups such as workers involuntarily separated due to plant closings or plan terminations. This policy would levy a benefit-related surcharge on plant closings and pension terminations.

If the government required employers to price index job-leaver benefits, employers might demand that the government provide an asset for funding these liabilities. Inflation-dependent deferred vested liabilities would add a new risk to the financial risks borne by the firm. There are currently no U.S. assets with values that match the fluctuations in that liability. If the government issued indexed bonds—bonds whose rate of return is the inflation rate plus a stipulated real interest rate—that asset would eliminate the inflation risk that firms would otherwise bear in funding the liability for indexed deferred annuities.

Wage Indexing

An alternative approach to price indexing would require plans to index preretirement earnings for wage growth, as does social security. That indexing would cost firms more because wages generally rise faster than prices.

Requiring plans to index salaries in benefit calculations would not affect liabilities for workers who immediately retire at job separation. However, liabilities for deferred annuities—amounts a plan must pay employees who leave before the plan's early retirement age—could increase greatly.

Instead of indexing for actual inflation or actual wage growth, deferred pensions could be indexed for expected inflation or expected wage growth. This would reduce the financial risk to the firm because its liability would be certain. The firm's risk falls because the risk of future inflation has been shifted to workers. Depending on how high inflation actually is, such indexing may much exceed or fall far short of the amount needed to maintain the pension's real value.

Cost of Indexing

The Congressional Budget Office has estimated the cost of indexing the deferred vested benefits of job leavers. Plans that price-index benefits of job leavers up to retirement would have increases in annual costs ranging from 6 to 28 percent (Ozanne and Lindeman 1987). These costs equal 0.6 to 2.8 percent of annual compensation. If the policy only required indexed deferred annuities to be provided to job leavers with 10 or more years of work, the cost increase would be much smaller—4 to 19 percent. This expense may be viewed as small— roughly equal to one year's typical wage increase. However, the increase would be permanent. If increased costs were borne by workers as reduced wages, 0.4 to 2.8 percent of lifetime compensation, depending on the proposal, would permanently shift from wages to retirement benefits.

If benefits were indexed up to retirement to the Consumer Price Index, average portability losses (excluding those due to preretirement distributions) would decrease from 15 to 5 percent of pension wealth (table 9.2), and the share of the covered workforce experiencing such losses would fall from 59 to 41 percent (Hay/Huggins 1988). Only 3 percent of covered workers would lose over 19 percent of a full-career benefit.

Table 9.2
Portability Loss with Inflation Protection

Portability loss (%)	Percentage of covered workers	
	Current vesting requirements	Immediate vesting requirements
40 to 49	6.3	0.0
30 to 39	13.4	0.0
20 to 29	19.4	3.0
10 to 19	15.2	23.3
1 to 9	4.6	14.8
None	38.4	40.5
Gain	2.7	18.4
Total	100.0	100.0
Average loss for all workers	14.8	5.0
Average loss for workers with a loss	23.3	9.3

SOURCE: Hay/Huggins (1988).
NOTE: The portability loss is the percentage difference between the retirement benefit the worker would have received if all service had been covered by the retirement plan of the last employer and the benefit that the worker actually received. A worker who worked from at least age 30 to age 65 under one pension plan would not have a loss under this definition, since the maximum credited service for the plans in the model was 35 years. A worker who worked for 35 years under one plan and received a vested benefit from a second plan would show a "gain."

Indexing to general wage growth reduces benefit losses further. Such indexing would nearly eliminate portability losses for most workers. In the Hay/Huggins (1988) model, indexing vested pension benefits by general wage growth reduces average portability loss from 15 to 2 percent. For workers with losses, the average loss would fall from 23 to 5 percent (table 9.3). The Hay/Huggins model, however, excludes losses caused by lump sum distributions greater than $3,500.

Table 9.3
Portability Loss with Inflation and Productivity Protection

Portability loss (%)	Current vesting requirements	Immediate vesting requirements
	(Percentage of covered workers)	
40 to 49	6.3	0.0
30 to 39	13.4	0.0
20 to 29	19.4	0.0
10 to 19	15.2	2.8
1 to 9	4.6	17.3
None	38.4	38.2
Gain	2.7	41.7
Total	100.0	100.0
Average loss for all workers	14.8	1.5
Average loss for workers with a loss	23.3	5.0

SOURCE: Hay/Huggins (1988).
NOTE: The portability loss is the percentage difference between the retirement benefit the worker would have received if all service had been covered by the retirement plan of the last employer and the benefit that the worker actually received. A worker who worked from at least age 30 to age 65 under one pension plan would not have a loss under this definition, since the maximum credited service for the plans in the model was 35 years. A worker who worked for 35 years under one plan and received a vested benefit from a second plan would show a "gain."

The tax revenue consequences of this option are uncertain. Employers might adjust to the option by reducing overall benefit levels. Workers, bearing the costs through lower wages, shift compensation from immediately taxable wages to pension compensation nontaxable until paid as benefits. That shift sets the upper bound of revenue loss. If firms accommodated the change by decreasing other aspects of pension benefits or other nontaxable compensation, no revenue would be lost.

Service Credit

An option eliminating plan design portability losses would require the final employer to credit all service from previous employers with a pension. The final employer would pay the part of the benefit in excess of vested benefits from other employers. For a worker employed 20 years by each of two employers, both providing a benefit of 1.5 percent of the high-five average salary times years of work, the retirement benefit to be paid from the pension plan of the second employer would be paid as follows (Hay/Huggins 1988):

1. High-five average salary with first employer	$25,000
2. Benefit for 20 years from first employer's plan	$7,500
3. High-five average salary with second employer	$97,000
4. Benefit for 20 years from second employer's plan	$29,100
5. Benefit for 40 years from second employer's plan	$58,200
6. Second employer benefit if all service credited ((5) minus (2))	$50,700

Under current pension law, the second employer provides a benefit of $29,100. The worker loses benefits of 37 percent, because he/she receives a combined benefit of $36,600 rather than $58,200. If the second employer credited all service, the second employer would pay a benefit of $50,700 and no benefits would be lost. This proposal only benefits employees who go to a second employer who has a pension plan.

Both preretirement indexing and transfer of service credits increase employer costs for a defined benefit plan. The first increases cost of workers leaving before retirement by requiring the initial employer to increase benefits for subsequent wage or price increases. The second increases the cost of hiring job leavers by requiring the last employer to pay benefits for service with prior employers.

Both approaches induce employers to be selective in whom they hire. The first might cause employers to avoid hiring young workers, seen as likely job leavers. Employers might hire fewer young women, viewing them as likely to change jobs more frequently than older women or men. The second approach might cause employers to avoid hiring older workers with past service to be credited. Hutchens (1986) has found that firms with pensions are less likely to hire older workers.

Portability Clearinghouse

A federal clearinghouse for retirement benefits could aid in asset transfers between plans or hold and invest assets of workers who have left pension-covered jobs. Those favoring a clearinghouse argue that a central administrative agency would ease administration of portability. Opponents argue that it would create a costly and unnecessary new agency or further burden existing agencies. Moreover, it would unnecessarily involve the federal government in the private sector by investing pension funds. Further, IRAs were created as an alternative to a clearinghouse.

Age-Weighted Profit-Sharing Plans

Some policies being considered for reasons other than enhancing portability may increase portability losses. An example is an age-weighted profit sharing plan.[4] Small employers frequently face the dilemma of reconciling their desire for tax-sheltered retirement savings and worker desire for current income. One proposal would allow employers to adopt plans to which they contribute more money for workers nearing retirement and less for younger workers.[5] An employer could do this with a defined contribution plan, where contributions increase with age or service.

LIMITING LUMP SUM DISTRIBUTIONS

The largest cause of benefit loss is the cashout of preretirement lump sum distributions by job changers. Most defined contribution plans allow preretirement distributions; except for small sums, most defined benefit plans do not, although they could and some evidence suggests that increasingly they are.

Prohibiting preretirement distributions would raise retirement benefits. It would raise administrative costs but would cost relatively little because no additional benefits would be required. A variation would allow preretirement cashouts if they were rolled over into another pension plan or an IRA. With such a requirement, defined contribution plans could be obligated to accept transfers of lump sum distributions from other plans.

Alternatives would permit, but discourage, preretirement distributions. Some would differentiate between treatment of employer and employee contributions. Employee contributions are common as elective deferrals for 401(k) plans.[6] One variation would allow preretirement cashouts of accumulated assets based on employee contributions only (including employee contributions to 401(k) plans). An alternative to requiring a pension plan to provide these options would deny tax deductibility by ending tax qualification for noncomplying plans. Another option would penalize workers instead of employers, increasing the excise tax on preretirement lump sum distributions from 10 to 20 percent. This policy would discourage workers from taking lump sum distributions, but preserve the option to do so. Employer- and employee-derived distributions could be taxed at different rates.

These proposals can be combined. The excise tax on preretirement distributions attributable to employee contributions could be raised, while benefits attributable to employer contributions could be locked-in until retirement age. To enhance flexibility for workers, individuals could retain the availability of loans and hardship distributions based on employer contributions. The resulting revenue from these tax-based proposals would offset the tax revenue lost from employees who decide not to take distributions.

Any proposal to prohibit or limit preretirement lump sum distributions costs the federal government tax revenue in the short run, because the government no longer receives the 10 percent excise tax and the income tax paid on the distributions. Such a change, however, would raise future tax revenue by postponing receipt and taxation of benefits.

Because lump sum benefit calculations are based on standard mortality tables, workers with lower than average life expectancy gain by taking benefits as a lump sum distribution rather than as an annuity over a shortened life expectancy. This may induce some workers to opt for lump sum distributions. While plans can require workers to have a doctor certify that they are in good health to qualify for a lump sum distribution, this is rarely done.

Policy Options for Rollovers

If defined benefit plans were required to accept benefit credits and assets from other plans, difficult administrative problems would arise.[7] Benefits to be transferred are calculated by figuring accrued benefits under the old plan and converting them into equal credit under a new and perhaps totally different benefit accrual structure. The actuarial assumptions and methods used to calculate present value of accrued benefits must be set with careful thought to ensure equity between old and new employers.

With the wide range of funding methods and assumptions used by plans, the amount the old employer had accumulated for the terminating employee would not equal the amount that the new employer needs to fund all past liabilities for that employee. The amount transferred would have to be a compromise between the accumulated liabilities under the old and new employers' actuarial methods and assumptions.

An employee in a single-employer pension plan rarely moves to a job with an identical plan. Thus, as well as determining which employer pays for the benefits the worker otherwise would have lost, the new employer must determine the service to be credited under the new plan. If the new plan is more generous than the old one, then the new plan would credit less service than the employee had previously worked. The lesser service rewarded at the more generous rate would give the equivalent benefit to that accrued under the old plan for more years of service rewarded at a lower rate.[8]

The present value of accrued liabilities is greatly affected by the actuarial assumptions used in the pension plan. For a plan with a normal retirement age of 65 and typical mortality and interest assumptions, a 1 percentage point increase in the interest rate lowers the accrued liability by approximately 25 percent for a worker age 40. For a worker age 20, a 1 percentage point increase decreases the accrued liability by 38 percent (Hay/Huggins 1990a). Changes in the annual salary increase assumption have a similarly large effect. A 1 percentage point increase in the salary growth rate assumption increases the accrued liability by 27 percent for a worker age 40 and increases it by

54 percent for a worker age 20. Actuaries do not have free rein in choosing assumptions, however, but are statutorily required to ensure that each is reasonable.

A solution to problems arising from plans using different actuarial assumptions requires that all plans use prescribed assumptions when dealing with portability transfers. If portability law requires no speci- fied set of assumptions, the amount transferred would vary widely. Plans would pick actuarial assumptions that limit losses due to the transfer in and out of workers, shifting the costs to other employers.

MANDATING UNIFORM PLAN FEATURES

Benefit loss could be reduced by requiring employers to provide pensions with specified features. Converting the pension system entirely to career-average defined benefit plans, some analysts have argued, would eliminate portability loss due to plan design. However, career-average defined benefit plans are periodically upgraded to offset inflation, and thus also cause job leavers to lose benefits due to infla- tion. Service portability could be achieved by using standardized bene- fit formulas, with employers crediting full service for all jobs.

Requiring Defined Contribution Plans

If all workers were enrolled in defined contribution plans with locked-in contributions, the portability problem would be solved. However, in nearly all countries with well-developed private pension systems, defined benefit plans cover more workers and provide greater benefits than do defined contribution plans (Turner and Dailey 1991), perhaps because firms are better ble to bear the investment risk.

If employers were required to replace defined benefit plans with defined contribution plans, more of total benefits would be paid to short-service workers and less to career workers. If an employer replaced a defined benefit plan that cost 10 percent of salary with a defined contribution plan, the retirement benefits for a full-career employee would have to be lowered by 30 percent to keep the cost of the plan at 10 percent for a typical group of workers (Bureau of National Affairs 1988).

Requiring Defined Contribution Coverage as an Option

Defined contribution plans are not the best coverage for all workers. Instead of requiring defined contribution coverage, the government could require employers to provide it as an alternative to defined benefit coverage.[9] Employees could then plan for job change by choosing a defined contribution plan. Another alternative would permit only workers with special need for job mobility (engineers, nurses, scientists or secretaries) to qualify for this option.

All employers could be required to offer salary reduction 401(k) plans to employees requesting them. This requirement would impose administrative costs and fiduciary duties on employers. However, under current law the administrative costs of qualified plans can be charged against employee accounts. Further, ERISA offers options, such as self-directed accounts for each employee, that could be used by employers to minimize fiduciary exposure.

MANDATING PENSIONS AND ALTERNATIVES

The Minimum Universal Pension System, proposed by the President's Commission on Pension Policy in 1980, would have required employers to contribute 3 percent of compensation to a defined contribution plan for each worker over age 25 who had been with the firm at least one year. Contributions would be immediately 100 percent vested. Employers preferring not to administer a pension plan would contribute to a portability clearinghouse, which would transfer funds to a central portability fund for investment. Those favoring this mandatory pension proposal argue that it would ensure a minimum benefit for all workers and provide a fully funded portable pension.

Proposals for mandating pensions may limit the requirement to employers hiring over a minimum number of workers, or by including only workers who work over a minimum number of hours a year. Mandating private pension coverage, however, conflicts with the voluntary nature of the U.S. private pension system. Moreover, critics argue that if a more expansive mandatory retirement system is desirable, it would be more efficient to expand social security rather than create a new entity. They also argue that the 3 percent payroll tax may hurt small and marginal businesses. Moreover, many low-income and young workers—those most likely to lack pension coverage—might not desire such a program if it resulted in lower cash wages. If the objective were to increase the retirement income of low-income workers, a more direct way of doing so would be to increase social security with its progressive benefit structure. Social security, however, is mostly unfunded, while a mandatory pension system would be fully funded.

Encouraging Increased Coverage

An alternative to mandating increased pension coverage would be to encourage coverage by offering attractive options to employers who adopt pension plans. Most large employers offer pensions, but many small employers do not. An option making pension provision more desirable to small employers exists in Japan, where small employers with pension plans receive a subsidy unavailable to large employers.

Another alternative would be to reduce the cost of pensions. The Internal Revenue Code and Title I of ERISA provide special treatment for Simplified Employee Pension plans (SEPs). A small employer who offers a SEP for which 25 or fewer employees qualify may offer a "cash or deferred arrangement" (CODA). These plans are commonly known as 408(k) plans. With these, the employee contributes by having the employer reduce his/her salary. In 1991, employees could contribute up to $8,475 to a SEP and reduce taxable income by the contribution. These plans may reduce the burden on employers because the employee makes the contribution.

One proposal for reducing portability losses by expanding coverage would raise the limit for employers who may offer SEP- CODAs to 50 eligible employees. The Department of Labor estimates that this proposal in 1990 could have extended plan coverage to 3.5 million workers in firms with 26 to 50 employees who were not covered by pension plans.

Increasing Availability of IRAs

Another way to address the disadvantages of short-service workers would be to increase their access to tax-favored savings independent of their employers. This change would also aid workers who are not already covered by an employer-provided pension plan. IRAs could be offered to all workers up to the defined contribution limit of 25 percent of earnings or $30,000. The increased availability of IRAs might encourage workers who change jobs to roll over pensions if they already were participating in an IRA.

Expanding Social Security

Social Security Old-Age and Survivors Insurance (OASI) provides fully portable benefits that are locked in until retirement. Credit for all social-security-covered employment is given when calculating benefit amounts. Thus, expanding social security, probably at the expense of employer-sponsored plans, would enhance portability. However, expanding mandatory social security would limit employer flexibility in designing compensation packages to meet worker needs.

NOTES

1. The Portability and Preservation of Pensions Work Group of the ERISA Advisory Council on Employee Welfare and Pension Benefit Plans.

2. The real interest rate is the rate of expected investment earnings less the expected rate of inflation. The result would be equivalent if expected and actual inflation were equal.

3. This discussion is taken largely from Ozanne and Lindeman (1987).

4. The material from this section is taken from Christl (1991).

5. This is proposed 401(a)(4) regulations from the U.S. Department of the Treasury.

6. With the exception of contributions to 401(k) plans, employee contributions to pension plans are not tax deductible. For this reason, employee contributions are treated differently in some proposals than are employer contributions.

7. These issues are discussed in Hay/Huggins (1990).

8. Assume that two plans have identical benefit structures except that the new plan provides a benefit at age 60 of 1.5 percent of final pay for each year of service, while the old plan provides a benefit at age 60 of 1.25 percent of final pay per year of service. For simplicity, assume that the worker's initial salary with the new employer equals his/her salary under the old employer: then 10 years of work under the old plan translates to 8.3 years under the new plan ($8.3=10 \times (1.25/1.5)$). If the worker qualified to receive the benefit at a younger age under the new plan than under the old one, the 8.3 years would be further reduced.

9. This proposal has been advanced by the Institute of Electrical and Electronics Engineers, Inc.

10

Portability Economics

Good public policy analysis must assess behavioral reactions, including the implications of policies for labor supply and demand, job quits, savings, investment, and other economic behaviors of workers and firms. Prior chapters examined potential costs of portability to firms. This chapter examines how pension portability affects behavior of workers and firms.

WHY FIRMS OFFER PENSIONS

Employers are less willing to offer pensions when portability policies reduce their advantages or raise their costs to firms. To anticipate how a policy will affect a firm and its workers requires understanding what firms gain by offering pensions.

The tax system encourages employers to provide pensions. Employer contributions are tax deductions for corporations and are untaxable personal income to workers. Returns earned on contributions also are untaxed as they accrue. The worker pays personal income taxes when he/she receives the benefits at retirement, but the marginal tax rate for most retirees is lower than their tax rate when working.

While it offers a rationale for why firms provide pensions, the tax system cannot explain why firms impose pension penalties on job changers. Pension penalties may aid firms by reducing turnover and increasing productivity, but these effects are absent in simple economic models where the labor market continuously equilibrates.[1] In these models, contemporaneous demand and supply set pay as if labor services were auctioned each period.

In such models, the only purpose for pay is to allocate workers to their most productive jobs; firms pay workers each period according to the value of the marginal product. Maximum labor market efficiency and national output result from the free flow of workers. In contrast, when jobs require firm-specific human capital, long job tenure raises efficiency by encouraging workers and firms to invest in worker skills.[2] Workers have firm-specific human capital when they have training that only increases their productivity with one employer. Workers who bear the full cost for training that raises their productivity only in their current firm suffer a capital loss from layoffs. But if the worker's wage with specific training is under the marginal value product, the firm also loses from a layoff.

For a firm to provide training, both worker and employer must have incentives to continue employment. The worker's wage must be above the alternative wage but below the value of the marginal product (Becker 1976). The optimal split of investment costs and returns between worker and firm depends on who is more likely to end the job, with that party being required to bear a larger cost. By sharing investment costs, a worker accepts reduced wages at an earlier age, causing wages to grow more rapidly with experience. This steepening of the wage profile encourages the worker to stay with the firm to receive higher wages later. The worker is induced to stay if the wage exceeds the current or projected alternative. Defined benefit pensions also encourage worker tenure, being deferred compensation with a value that increases with tenure.

Deferred pay also motivates workers in the "shirking" model. Employers may defer pay in jobs difficult to monitor, and in situations where workers are unproductive, steal, or otherwise shirk (Becker and Stigler 1974). Both worker and employer recognize that shirking is costly, and that reducing it benefits both parties by making workers more productive and raising their wages. A solution to shirking has the worker post "bond," forfeited if the employer detects shirking. While workers rarely post bond in cash, the firm may require workers to post bond by paying them under the value of marginal product early in their career and more than the marginal product value later. A terminated worker forfeits the bond (the deferred wages).

Pensions explicitly enter the shirking model (Lazear 1979). The pension separation penalty is like a bond. Workers sacrifice wages expecting to receive a pension based on work with the firm until retirement. If dismissed before retirement, they receive a pension valued at less than their implicit contributions via forgone wages. The difference between the wages they have forfeited and the lower pension they receive is the bond they forfeit.

Because of the tax structure, it is less costly to reduce turnover by backloading pensions than by deferring wages. Tilting the wage profile shifts taxable income from a low-tax-rate period—early tenure years, with lower income—to a high-tax-rate period—later working years with higher income. With a pension, however, compensation is shifted to retirement, when workers often face lower tax rates.[3] These marginal tax rate arguments are of greater economic importance during periods when the tax code is more progressive.

The human capital model and the shirking model justify long-tenure employment. The models may justify job separation penalties to provide incentives for long tenure, but in a dynamic economy some jobs should be temporary. The key question is whether the separation penalty in defined benefit plans raises productivity through long tenure or impedes efficient job mobility. To analyze the efficiency of mobility, consider an employment contract with firm-specific worker productivity. Worker and firm agree on an initial wage W. Both expect that the value of the marginal product will exceed the wage, which will exceed the worker's alternative wage. But, after the firm invests in the worker's productivity, that productivity rises for other reasons outside the firm. Now the worker's alternative wage exceeds the value of marginal product in the firm. The worker has an incentive to quit, but if he/she does, the firm loses its investment in the worker.

The firm requires the worker to pay via reduced wages for a "stay pension," which is the pension valued on the assumption that the worker will stay with the firm until retirement. If the worker quits, he/she must pay severance, which takes the form of portability loss, to compensate the firm for the lost training investment. The worker loses pension benefits if he/she quits, because the pension will be valued on current wage rather than projected wage at retirement.

If the worker loses pension benefits equal to the firm's loss on its investment in the worker, efficient quits are guaranteed. The worker quits only if capitalized earnings gained on the new job offset the pension benefits lost from the old one. Thus, quit penalties arising from nonportable pensions not only encourage investment in firm- specific capital, but also preserve efficient job matches under demand and supply shocks.

When a worker's productivity declines, the employer may wish to terminate him/her, but damage to an employer's reputation in the labor market may be sufficient to prevent that action. As an alternative, a firm could offer severance pay sufficient to offset lost wages plus reduced pension value. If that amount is less than the difference between the worker's wages and his/her value of marginal product, both worker and firm are better off.

Workers whose alternative value of marginal product exceeds their wage prefer to change jobs, but by discharge (rather than resignation) to avoid the quit penalty. They have an incentive to reduce current productivity to cause that result. Similarly, a firm wishing to lay off a worker has an incentive to create working conditions that prompt the worker to quit. An implicit contract creating such incentives would reduce worker productivity and is in neither side's interest.

Such moral hazard problems, however, would be mitigated by limiting severance payments to major layoffs such as plant closings. The Pension Benefit Guaranty Corporation (PBGC) has liabilities of over $1 billion due to plant closing benefits (Lockhart 1990), providing evidence on the extent that these benefits are offered. These liabilities were 25 percent of PBGC claims in 1990, mostly for collectively bargained plant-closing benefits in the steel and automobile industries. In some U.S. plans workers have shorter vesting schedules or are credited with extra years of work if job ending is due to layoff. In Japan, pension benefits are generally higher for laid-off workers than for voluntary job leavers.

In sum, a nonportable defined benefit pension may act as an efficient severance tax, discouraging excessive quits. When conditions call for layoffs, however, the employer must pay severance to the worker to honor the implicit contract and not lose reputation in the labor market. But given problems in calculating sufficient severance pay, portability loss may impede efficient firm-initiated separations.

PENSIONS AND TURNOVER

This book has examined how job change causes workers to lose pension benefits. Now the reverse is examined: How does pension benefit loss affect the odds that a worker will change jobs?

Empirical studies have produced overwhelming statistical evidence that pensions correlate with reduced worker turnover. In addition to vesting, which has already been discussed, three factors contribute to that correlation. First, pension benefits are often backloaded, rewarding long tenure. Second, workers who are inherently less likely to quit or be fired—"stayers"—may prefer jobs offering pensions more than do workers more likely to change jobs—"movers." Third, jobs with pensions often offer higher wages than those found elsewhere, reducing quits and thus reducing turnover.

Backloading

Defined benefit plans are backloaded. This means benefits—relative to earnings—accrue more rapidly the nearer the worker is to retirement, or the more years he/she has worked. While ERISA limits backloading by requiring vesting after a fixed period and by restricting pension benefit formulas, it permits some backloading in benefit formulas.

Backloading occurs in a benefit formula by raising pension accrual with age or service or by making options available to workers who leave the firm at retirement age and unavailable to workers leaving earlier. Career-average benefit formulas can be backloaded by giving more credit for later service in computing the average. More commonly, benefit formulas are backloaded by being based on final salary. The federal Civil Service Retirement System, for example, uses a backloaded benefit formula.[4] It provides annual benefit accrual of 1.5 percent for the first five years of work, 1.75 percent for the next five years, and 2 percent beyond the first 10 years, the percentage applying to the average of the three consecutive years of highest salary.

Backloading also occurs by giving higher postretirement cost-of-living adjustments to retirees with greater years worked, or higher adjustments to retirees who stayed with the firm until retirement age. It occurs by giving employees who work until the early retirement age the option of receiving benefits earlier than employees who leave the firm at younger ages. Backloading rewards workers with steep earnings profiles, and it thus can be used by firms to reward successful workers with positions of responsibility.

Final-salary defined benefit plans are implicitly backloaded because they are tied to end-of-job salary. In 1989, 64 percent of participants in defined benefit plans in large and medium-size firms were in plans using final-salary formulas (Mitchell 1992). However, most other defined benefit plans are implicitly tied to final salary through *ad hoc* adjustments in benefit formulas to keep pace with wages.

Backloading occurs in some defined contribution plans, for example those that distribute forfeited nonvested benefits of early leavers to remaining participants based on account balances. This procedure rewards long-tenure workers due to their large account balances.

Integrating pension benefits with social security causes backloading. Because workers typically have higher earnings later in life, benefit formulas with higher accrual rates at higher earnings back load. Social security integration causes backloading because pension accrual rates are higher for workers earning above the social security taxable maximum earnings. Companies may integrate both defined contribution and defined benefit plans with social security.

How common is explicit backloading? In 1989, 46 percent of workers in defined benefit plans with final-salary formulas were in plans where the accrual rate explicitly varied by service, age, or earnings (table 10.1). The comparable figure for workers in plans with career-average formulas is 59 percent, and when that formula is integrated with social security the figure is 95 percent. In flat-dollar benefit formulas, the benefit per year of service varies by earnings or service for 17 percent of participants. In deferred profit-sharing plans of large and medium-size firms in 1989, 9 percent of participants were in plans varying the accrual rate based on service (table 10.2). Thus the view that defined contribution plans are never explicitly backloaded is false. Backloading through integration with social security is also common among plans offered by large and medium-size firms (table 10.3). In 1989, 63 percent of participants in these plans were in integrated plans. This percentage varied greatly by plan type. For final-salary and career-average plans, 86 percent and 62 percent of participants, respectively, were in integrated plans, while under 0.5 percent of participants in flat-dollar plans were in integrated plans.

Backloading also occurs through higher cost-of-living adjustments to retirees with long tenure (Allen, Clark, and McDermed 1992). For workers in large and medium-size firms receiving a postretirement benefit increase during 1984-88, 24 percent were in plans where the increase depended on years worked.

Table 10.1
Percentage of Full-Time Participants in Defined Benefit Plans
Where the Benefit Formula Varies
by Service, Age, or Earnings, 1989

	Terminal earnings benefit formulas		Career earnings benefit formulas	
	Total	With integrated formula	Total	With integrated formula
Percent per year varies	46	53	59	95
By service	16	17	4	3
By earnings	24	30	43	71
By age	3	3	a	a
By earnings and service	3	3	12	20
Dollar amount benefit formula				
Amount per year of services varies	17			
By earnings	15			
By service	2			

SOURCE: U.S. Department of Labor (1990), pp. 89, 92.
a. Less than 0.5 percent.

Table 10.2
Percentage of Full-Time Participants in Deferred
Profit-Sharing Plans Where the Allocation Varies
by the Participants' Earnings or Service
1986, 1988, 1989

Type of formula	Percent of full-time participants		
	1986	1988	1989
Employer contributions			
(1) Based on stated formula	59	55	60
Fixed percent of profits	NA	16	10
Variable percent of profits	NA	12	18
Other formulas	NA	27	33
(2) No formula	41	45	40
Allocation of profits to employees			
Equally to all	1	1	1
Based on earnings	61	74	64
Based on earnings and service	10	12	9
Other	8	13	26
Loans from employees' accounts			
Permitted	25	32	19
Not permitted	75	68	81

SOURCE: U.S. Department of Labor, Bureau of Labor Statistics (1990).
NOTES: Data exclude supplemental pension plans. Sums may not equal totals because of rounding. NA means data not available.

147

Table 10.3
Percentage of Full-Time Participants in Defined Benefit Plans that Integrate, 1980-1989

Type of formula	Percent of full-time participants								
	1980	1981	1982	1983	1984	1985	1986	1988	1989
Without integrated formula	55	57	55	45	44	39	38	38	37
With integrated formula	45	43	45	55	56	61	62	62	63
Benefit offset by SS payment*	30	33	35	35	36	40	43	39	41
Excess formula**	16	10	10	20	20	27	24	26	24

SOURCE: Mitchell (1992).
NOTES: Data exclude supplemental pension plans. Sums may not equal totals because of rounding.
*Pension benefit calculated is reduced by a portion of primary social security payments.
**Pension formula applies lower benefit rate to earnings subject to social security taxes or below a specified dollar threshold.

Measuring Backloading

ERISA limits explicit backloading, trying to assure that benefits accrue steadily over a worker's career. But even if a defined benefit formula weighs equally all years so that it is not explicitly backloaded, considerable backloading occurs in most of the formulas.

Backloading in a defined benefit plan can be measured as follows. First, calculate the constant contribution rate needed for a defined contribution plan to equal the defined benefit plan's value at the projected retirement date. Next, figure the current value of this hypothetical defined contribution plan. This current value measures the value the defined benefit plan would have accrued were it not backloaded. The gap between this value and the defined benefit plan's current value measures backloading.[5]

Assume, for simplicity, that the benefit formula is 1 percent times final salary times years worked, with immediate vesting. The worker joins a firm at age 40 with a salary of $100,000, so that the first year of work adds $1,000 to his/her annual benefit at retirement. By age 50 the worker has a salary of $200,000 and adds $2,000 to his annual benefit at retirement (1 percent x $200,000). But because this salary is higher than his/her age 49 salary, and because he/she now has already worked 10 years, 1 percent times 10 times the difference between his/her salary of $200,000 and his/her salary at 49, say $190,000, is also added. This is another $1,000; that is, the prior year the future annual retirement benefit equaled 1 percent times 10 years times $190,000. This year the future annual retirement benefit equals 1 percent times 11 years times $200,000. The greater annual retirement benefits gained by working another year at age 50 are caused by the added year of service and the higher salary interacted with past service. The total rise is $3,000.

Assume the worker's salary rose from $100,000 at age 40 to $200,000 at age 50 because the price level doubled. (This occurs with 7 percent inflation.) In real dollars, the worker's salary is equal in both years, being $200,000 in age-50 dollars. But his/her year of work at age 40 raised the nominal benefits at retirement by $1,000 (or 0.5 percent of real salary), while his/her year of work at age 50 raised the nominal benefits at retirement by $3,000 (or 1.5 percent of salary). Thus, for equal real salary, his/her year of work at age 50 had three times as large an effect on annual benefits at retirement. With no inflation, the same salary pattern provides a much smaller increase in pension accrual relative to salary. With no inflation—the worker's salary rising from $100,000 to $200,000 solely due to greater productivity— pension accrual rises from 1 percent of real wages to 1.5 percent.

This example demonstrates how typical defined benefit pension formulas backload benefit accruals. It also shows how the degree of backloading depends heavily on inflation. But it understates backloading by ignoring interest discounting, which reduces the value of pension accruals early in life relative to those late in life. It also understates the difference in the two examples, because in the inflation example the discounting would be greater due to the increase in the nominal interest rate. These calculations also understate backloading by ignoring the effect of awarding greater percentage cost-of-living adjustments to retirees with long careers and by assuming no explicit backloading.

Backloading has a disadvantage to employers as a job-tenure incentive: it is heavily influenced by inflation, which employers do not control. Why would employers want job leavers to lose more when inflation is higher? This arrangement may be a second-best solution because ERISA limits the extent to which benefit formulas explicitly backload (Ippolito 1986a). With no economic reason why mobility should be lower when inflation is high, it would appear that during inflationary periods some workers may be discouraged from quitting when it otherwise would be efficient to do so.

Backloading and Job Change

The effect of backloading on job change depends on the underlying employment contract. Pensions impose a penalty on early separations when firms implicitly promise workers a job until retirement—an "implicit lifetime contract" (Ippolito 1985). The term describes the unstated but implied promises a firm makes about future benefits and employment. The contract takes this form because explicit agreements on future employment are rarely made. Exceptions occur predominantly in collectively bargained agreements.

Implicit contracts regarding future benefits are not legally enforceable. For that reason, and because later they may conflict with the firm's interest, implicit contracts must have an economic rather than legal enforcement mechanism for workers to rely on. To be viable and retain credibility, they must be self-enforcing. It must be in each party's long-run interest to maintain the contract, though it may not always be in each party's short-run interest.

With an implicit contract, at least one party's earnings must exceed the best alternative. Two potential sources of surplus in the employment relationship are the productivity gains of job-specific human capital and the savings in direct mobility costs for each party if they need not find new partners.

The crucial factor in long-term implicit contracts is a firm's ability to credibly commit itself. If the firm violates implicit contracts, it will be unable to exercise this option in the future and will lose the benefits of raised productivity. The firm will also have more difficulty in hiring workers. Because larger firms fail less and may care more about reputation in the labor market, larger firms more commonly make implicit contracts.

Implicit contracts may explain why larger firms offering pensions grant *ad hoc* cost-of-living adjustments to retirees, though they are not legally or contractually obligated to do so. It may also explain why firms with low predicted failure rates, and thus more credible implicit contracts, more commonly offer pensions (Curme and Kahn 1990).

A backloaded pension does not affect job change if the worker expects to leave the employer long before retirement. The worker only gives up wages in exchange for a pension based on current earnings, which are lower than final earnings. This labor market, where the worker is only hired for one period at a time, is called a spot market. It is also characterized as the legal view of the market because firms are only legally obligated to provide pension accrual based on current worker earnings (Bulow 1982).

In a spot labor market, a worker's current wage equals his/her marginal productivity. The worker realizes that layoff may occur due to bankruptcy or decreased demand for the firm's product; the firm realizes that the worker may find a better job and leave. Thus, both parties require full pay in each period, with the wage being constantly renegotiated as labor market conditions change. When workers change jobs in a spot market they lose nothing, though their pension benefits are lower than otherwise, because they have not paid for those benefits through forgone wages. Thus, though their future benefits are reduced, with no capital loss workers are not discouraged from changing jobs.

Gustman and Steinmeier (1987) compare the spot market value of pension accrual to pension accrual with continued employment. For workers age 25 to 34 with tenure up to 10 years, the accrual based on the spot market assumption averaged 0.6 percent of earnings, versus 14.1 percent for employment to retirement. At ages 45 to 54 with 21 to 30 years worked, the two averages were 10.4 and 15.8 percent. The diminishing gap between the two averages indicates backloading.

The amount a job leaver loses in pension benefits under a long-tenure implicit contract depends on the worker's age and tenure. The pension portability loss curve over a lifetime is hill shaped, rising and then falling as age of separation rises. Low service and earnings cause the pension portability loss initially to be low, but it grows with tenure due to rising accrued benefits. Under a wide variety of assumptions, the loss peaks around age 45 or 50 and then declines. The decline occurs because the gap between separation earnings and retirement age earnings shrinks, offsetting the rising accrued benefits against which a loss is suffered. The portability loss falls to zero at retirement age.

Allen, Clark, and McDermed (1988) estimate that job leavers age 40 to 55 generally lose benefits equal to between one-half and two-thirds of annual earnings. Considering the time over which workers recoup these losses through higher earnings at alternative employment, the capital loss could be a powerful impediment to job change for older workers. Further, for firms caring about their reputation as employers, the capital loss also results in fewer layoffs because layoffs reduce retirement benefits for workers.

Kotlikoff and Wise (1987) calculate how much pension wealth workers lose when changing jobs and compare that to the workers' expected future wages. Their calculations range from 2 to 50 percent of future wages, depending on age of hire, normal retirement age, and age of job change. Most losses are less than 10 percent, but they vary by plan. A worker starting work at age 31 and changing jobs at age 41 has accrued for that period on average only 72 percent of the pension wealth of a worker staying with the firm until retirement.

Sorting

The sorting hypothesis provides another explanation for why workers with pensions tend to have long job tenure. The sorting hypothesis states that firms use pension plans to select workers least likely to leave. If some workers are "stayers" while others are "movers," the firm has an incentive to sort out movers. A bonus conditional on long-term attachment is worth less to a mover, or to a person with a low discount rate, and will thus achieve the desired goal (Salop and Salop 1976). Such a bonus improves the firm's productivity because by attracting low turnover workers the firm's search, hiring, and training costs are reduced. Without deferred pay, workers have little incentive to consider how job change affects their employer.

Some analysts criticize this theory because defined benefit plans are inefficient in screening out quitters at hire. For firms where training costs occur at the beginning of employment, turnover shortly after hire is the most costly. Defined benefit plans lightly penalize short-tenure workers; however, for firms who train workers over a long period, pensions may be effective.

Efficiency Wages

Another reason for the correlation between pensions and long job tenure involves an employer's use of additional compensation to encourage long tenure. One such aspect of compensation has been called "efficiency wages." Some analysts argue that pension jobs pay high wages to deter worker turnover. According to this argument, the high wages rather than features of pension plans are the cause of the correlation between pensions and low job turnover.

STATISTICAL STUDIES

Studies have demonstrated that pension coverage negatively correlates with reduced turnover, quits, and layoffs[6] and is positively related to tenure.[7] Two studies investigate how pensions affect worker job mobility by modeling the impact of vesting standards—Schiller and Weiss (1979) and Wolf and Levy (1984). Neither study estimates the value of benefits job leavers lose.

Schiller and Weiss (1979) hypothesized that workers considering job change compare the discounted value of wages and pensions on the current job to the discounted value of those streams of compensation on alternative jobs. They found that higher values of unvested benefits reduced the odds of job change, and that vested workers were more likely to change jobs. They found that workers age 25 to 39 in plans with longer vesting periods had higher odds of quitting before vesting. Because they used pre-ERISA data, some plans may have required over 10 years for vesting.

Wolf and Levy (1984) examined the relationship between pension coverage, pension vesting rules, and job tenure. They found the odds of leaving a job with 10-year vesting are four times greater the year after vesting than the year before.

With ERISA rules, pension accruals are small at vesting so workers of most ages lose little due to job change during early years of work on a job (Kotlikoff and Wise 1985, 1987). For workers vesting at older ages due to having started working on a pension-covered job later in life, being unvested reduces job change more. This may be due to backloading, which would cause the unvested benefits of older workers to be greater than for younger workers.

Using a sample of 1,000 pension plans, and using intermediate wage and interest rate assumptions, Kotlikoff and Wise found that the pension wealth gain for those vesting at age 40 is 14 percent of annual earnings for 10-year vesting. The pension wealth gain is much larger for workers vesting at later ages—36 percent at 50 and 66 percent at age 60. Ten-year vesting is now banned in single- employer plans, but permitted in multiemployer plans. The gains are smaller with five-year vesting; nonetheless, vesting could be important in reducing the mobility of older workers before they attain vesting. Studies thus find that vesting reduces mobility for workers approaching the vesting limit.

Mitchell (1982) examined effects of pension coverage on job turnover and found that a male worker with a pension plan quit 10 percent less frequently than his counterpart without a plan. She also found that higher wages reduced job change.

Monitoring theories of compensation predict that pensions at small firms will be less backloaded and have a smaller impact on the quit rate of workers than pensions at large firms. This prediction is based on the assumption that smaller firms are better able to monitor their workers and do not as much need to use deferred compensation as an incentive device. Further, firms with backloaded pensions may honor promises of deferred compensation by offering a lower risk of permanent layoff. If small firms do not backload pensions to reduce turnover, their pensions should have a smaller effect on quits and layoffs. Even and Macpherson (1990a) test these implications of monitoring theories. They find quits and job changes are more likely to occur at small firms. Between 1983 and 1986, the quit and job change rates are 26 and 39 percent at small firms, but 15 and 24 percent at large firms. Estimating a probit model of quits and job changes shows that pensions do not affect quits or job changes at small firms, but affect both at large firms.

This pattern may occur because defined contribution plans are more common at small firms. Bodie and Papke (1990) and others have found that defined contribution plans are less costly for small firms than are defined benefit plans. Dorsey (1987) shows that small firms choose defined contribution over defined benefit plans even after controlling for worker and industry attributes.

In a second empirical specification, Even and Macpherson (1990a) test whether the mobility effect depends on which plan is in use— defined benefit or defined contribution. The results show that neither plan reduces mobility at small firms, whereas both reduce mobility at large firms. This supports the prediction that larger firms, being more concerned with labor turnover, more commonly design pensions to impede mobility, but leaves unanswered why defined contribution plans have this effect

The next two studies concentrate on the benefits workers lose due to backloading in defined benefit plans. Both studies estimate the dollar value of losses. Allen, Clark and McDermed (1990) found that stayers seek jobs offering pension coverage, and that sorting of workers associates pensions with reduced turnover. Backloading pension benefit accruals had less effect, and reduced layoffs more than quits. These results suggest that policy changes for calculating vesting or benefits are unlikely to raise labor mobility.

In contrast, Gustman and Steinmeier (1990) argue that the wage premium on pension jobs explains most of the reduced mobility of pension-covered workers. They marshal evidence suggesting that backloading does not cause the correlation between pension coverage and long job tenure. First, for workers in their early forties and younger, the loss from backloading is a small part of compensation, so that workers gaining from a move easily offset the pension benefits they lose. Second, estimates of mobility equations show the puzzling finding that defined contribution plans, generally not backloaded, reduce turnover as much as defined benefit plans. This result suggests that backloading does not cause lower turnover rates. Finally, when a compensation premium measure is included in the mobility equation, the compensation premium measure and not backloading accounts for most of the difference in mobility rates between pension- and nonpension-covered workers. Their results suggest that benefit backloading is statistically significant in reducing worker mobility, but has a small effect.

Gustman and Steinmeier (1990) used data on males age 31 to 50 working at least 30 hours a week in private sector, nonagricultural jobs from the 1984 panel of the Survey of Income and Program Participation (SIPP). They found that of workers who left jobs voluntarily, 59 percent were in nonpension jobs, while 43 percent had held pension jobs.[8] The accuracy of these statistics was unclear, however, because of data problems concerning reasons for job leaving. Using a different data set—the Panel Study of Income Dynamics (PSID), with 1984 data—Gustman and Steinmeier find that 64 percent of nonpension-covered workers and 61 percent of pension-covered workers were voluntary job movers.

Both data sets have weaknesses that reduce reliability. Further, the number of involuntary job leavers with pensions rises during economic downturns, so that a single statistic for a short period does not reflect a business cycle. While complete data on voluntary and involuntary job change for pension-covered workers are unavailable, the available data show that involuntary job leavers are an important aspect of the pension portability issue.

Gustman and Steinmeier (1990) find individuals initially without pensions are over three times more likely (19.5 versus 6.1 percent) to change jobs than individuals with pensions. The gap between movers from pension and nonpension jobs is even wider when coverage in the new jobs is considered. Of movers from nonpension jobs, 14 percent gained pensions, while 64 percent of movers from pension jobs lost coverage in the move. Pension figures for the new job include only workers in a pension plan as of the 1985 survey. If you include those excluded because they "have not worked for the employer long enough," the share of movers from nonpension jobs who gained pensions rises to 21 percent, and the share of movers from pension jobs losing pensions drops to 56 percent (table 10.4).[9]

The figures for those who lost pension coverage in a job change show a far different reality from what is commonly assumed. The Hay/Huggins (1988) study of portability assumed that job leavers with pensions went to jobs with pensions. The study bases the assumption on the hypothesis of two worker types: (1) lower-income workers receiving adequate social security benefits to maintain their living standard and thus never covered by a pension; and (2) higher-income workers needing a pension to supplement social security benefits in retirement and thus covered by a pension. The statistics from the Gustman and Steinmeier study show that many workers leaving pension jobs take nonpension jobs.

Gustman and Steinmeier figure the value of backloading versus projected compensation for pension-covered workers. Backloading is expressed in dollars per hour of work until retirement because the worker must stay until retirement to avoid losing the backloaded benefits. This is compared to cumulative wages until retirement, again in dollars per hour until retirement. They find backloading averages only 2.5 percent of projected compensation for pension-covered workers. This represents 21 percent of pension wealth for the workers in this sample.[10] In the empirical estimations, they find backloading accounts for 5 percent of the difference in mobility rates between pensioned workers and nonpensioned workers. For workers age 45 to 50, backloading accounts for 8 percent of the difference in mobility rates between pension- and nonpension-covered workers.

The results of Gustman and Steinmeier thus imply that making pensions perfectly portable would have little effect on job tenure for most pension-covered workers. They conclude that pension coverage is associated with efficiency wages that are higher than market wages. Pension-covered workers generally have a higher wage on the current

Table 10.4
Wages, Pensions, and Mobility, 1984

	Stayers	Movers
	No pension in 1984 job	
Percent movers	19.5% (998)	
Mean wage in 1984	$8.71 (654)	$7.72 (133)
Mean wage in 1985	$8.86 (654)	$8.23 (133)
Percent with 1985 pension		13.8% (160)
	Pension in 1984 job	
Percent movers	6.1% (1753)	
Mean wage in 1984	$11.87 (1490)	$11.22 (88)
Mean wage in 1985	$11.89 (1490)	$10.52 (88)
Percent with 1985 pension		35.8% (107)
	Defined benefit pension in 1984 job	
Percent movers	6.0% (1126)	
Mean wage in 1984	$11.95 (960)	$11.94 (58)
Mean wage in 1985	$11.94 (960)	$10.81 (58)
Percent with 1985 pension		42.9% (63)
	Defined contribution pension in 1984 job (including profit-sharing plans)	
Percent movers	6.2% (627)	
Mean wage in 1984	$11.73 (530)	$9.94 (30)

Table 10.4 (continued)
Wages, Pensions, and Mobility, 1984

	Stayers	Movers
Mean wage in 1985	$11.82 (530)	$9.96 (30)
Percent with 1985 pension		21.9% (32)
Defined contribution pension in 1984 job (excluding profit-sharing plans)		
Percent movers	6.9% (174)	
Mean wage in 1984	$11.53 (149)	$12.03 (8)
Mean wage in 1985	$11.44 (149)	$10.70 (8)
Percent with 1985 pension		22.2% (9)

SOURCE: Gustman and Steinmeier (1990).

NOTES: Figures in parentheses are numbers of observations. Wages are indexed to 1984 dollars by the Index of Average Hourly Earnings (1989 Economic Report of the President, table B-44) and are included in the means only if valid wage observations are available in both years. Means are geometric means (i.e., antilogs of mean log wages). Wages less than $1 or greater than $50 are excluded from the analysis.

job than that attainable from the next best job. That wage premium reduces turnover and may help to explain the reduced turnover ascribed to pension coverage.

EFFICIENCY EFFECTS OF PENSIONS

Econometric studies suggest that pensions reduce mobility for some workers, particularly older workers in large firms. Less attention has been paid to the effect of pension-reduced mobility on labor market efficiency.[11]

Whether a defined benefit pension raises labor market efficiency is an empirical question hinging on whether the quit penalty in the pension is systematically related to the value a firm places on long job tenure. While the quit penalty may be explained as a tool to reduce inefficient quits, evidence is needed to support that contention. If the amount of benefits workers lose is unrelated to training, monitoring costs, or the need to attract stable workers, the result will be inefficiency due to reduced labor market flexibility.

Deferred compensation reduces worker shirking. Thus firms are likely to use that tactic when direct monitoring of worker effort would be costly. It follows that jobs where monitoring costs are high are more likely to offer pensions. Hutchens (1987) found that jobs classified as repetitive in the Dictionary of Occupational Titles had a 9 percentage point lower probability of pension coverage than other jobs. Further, jobs classified as repetitive strongly correlated with a Dictionary of Occupational Titles measure of the time required to obtain the skills needed for the jobs. When this training index is added to the pension coverage equation, the estimated coefficient on training is positive and large. This finding supports the argument that pension-induced long tenure raises the benefit from firm-specific training.

Dorsey (1990) investigated the relationship between the required training for a job and pension coverage and provides evidence that pension coverage is associated with training.[12] This presumably occurs by reducing quits, so that the firm can count on recouping training expenses. In another study, Dorsey (1987) used IRS data on pension plan sponsors to estimate the causes of primary defined benefit versus defined contribution coverage. If nonportability raises worker productivity, firms with production processes requiring greater training or monitoring should be more likely to provide defined benefit coverage. Dorsey's estimates show that industries with high concentrations of professional, managerial, and craftsmen occupations were more likely to have defined benefit pensions.

In sum, indirect evidence is consistent with a correlation between pensions and increased productivity. The pattern of pension coverage supports predictions from the training and shirking models, where pensions have a productivity augmenting role. Moreover, some initial direct evidence shows that pension coverage occurs more commonly in firms providing greater training. Finally, employers are more reluctant to discharge workers facing a high pension separation penalty. This result suggests that employers have valuable investments in those workers.

POLICY IMPLICATIONS

Reducing the vesting period from five years is likely to have little effect on job change except for short-tenure workers, who may be induced to stay on the job long enough to vest when the vesting period is reduced. After vesting, the odds of job change rise, so that reducing the vesting period may ultimately increase job change. Indexing deferred vested benefits for inflation would also raise mobility, for the same reason. But imposing standards to guarantee benefit preservation—prevent preretirement cashouts—might reduce mobility because workers could not access pension assets by changing jobs.

Gustman and Steinmeier (1990) argue that raising portability by reducing the benefits workers lose due to backloading would little affect job change, because backloading has little effect on job change. Allen, Clark, and McDermed (1990) agree, but from a different premise. They argue that there would be little effect on job change because backloading, for the most part, reduces layoffs, an effect examined more closely in the next chapter. If either argument is correct, reducing backloading would not affect job change.

NOTES

1. This discussion largely follows Dorsey (1990).

2. This theory was pioneered by Gary Becker (1964) and Walter Oi (1962).

3. There are also tax advantages to employers for deferring compensation through pensions, rather than deferring by paying higher wages later. The returns on employer contributions to a pension plan are not taxed while they accrue. However, if the employer had funded deferred wages by investing in the firm, the retained earnings invested in the firm would not be tax deductible, and the returns on the capital in the firm would be taxed at the marginal corporate income tax rate.

4. The Civil Service Retirement System is unregulated by ERISA.

5. This method of calculating backloading, used by Gustman and Steinmeier (1990), is a generalization of the method used by Ippolito (1986a).

6. These studies have been surveyed in Andrews (1990) and Gustman and Mitchell (1991).

7. See for instance Wolf and Levy (1984).

8. The Census Bureau regards these data as preliminary and requires the following statement regarding their use: "This report uses data from the Survey of Income and Program Participation 1984 Panel (Preliminary) Wave 6 Core plus Topical Module File, which was released by the Census Bureau for research to improve understanding and analysis of SIPP data. The data on the file are preliminary and should be analyzed and interpreted with caution. At the time the file was created, the Census Bureau was still exploring certain unresolved technical and methodological issues associated with the creation of this data set. The Census Bureau does not approve or endorse the use of these data for official estimates."

9. The percentage of job movers who had a pension on a previous job but not on the current job is higher than Piacentini (1990b) found, but the Piacentini results are for movers who had a pension on any previous job, while the Gustman and Steinmeier results are only for a one-year time period.

10. The magnitude of the backloading loss found by Gustman and Steinmeier (1990) is consistent with that found by Allen, Clark, and McDermed (1990).

11. This discussion is drawn largely from Dorsey (1990).

12. He uses data from the Panel Study of Income Dynamics.

II

Layoffs and Portability Issues

This chapter examines the relationship between pensions, pension portability, and layoffs and focuses on two interrelated policy issues: the impact of pensions on layoffs and the reverse impact of layoffs on pension benefits. The discussion of these issues suggests that special portability policies may be needed to aid workers who are laid off.[1]

THE IMPACT OF PENSIONS ON LAYOFFS

There are two ways in which pensions could affect layoffs. First, firms that offer pensions could engage in the opportunistic behavior of laying off pensioned workers more readily than nonpensioned workers. Opportunistic behavior could also be in evidence when firms that offer pension coverage exhibit higher layoff rates than firms that do not offer pension coverage. There could be financial gain for the firm from laying off unvested workers or from laying off older workers who are covered by defined benefit plans and who have not yet reached the age of benefit eligibility. (Backloading of pension liabilities creates an incentive for firms to dismiss this latter group of workers.) Such actions, however, may violate pension law.

Second, pensions could discourage layoffs, either because of some feature of a plan that inhibits layoff or some characteristic of pension-covered jobs or the workers in these jobs that is also associated with low layoff rates. Theories to explain this effect vary widely.

Opportunistic Behavior by Firms

Firms engaged in opportunistic behavior, for example, when they offer pensions to workers whom they intend to dismiss long before the workers can collect the full value of their pension benefits. While there may be financial gain for firms from this behavior, there are reputational costs to consider.[2] Firms can also hire workers with the intent of fulfilling pension obligations, but then dismiss them prematurely because of unexpected change in the firm's situation (e.g., a technological breakthrough or unexpected foreign competition). Again, this can result in financial gains to the firm. In both cases, whether behaving in a deceptive manner or responding to an unexpected change, the firm is said to be engaging in opportunistic behavior.

Most of the evidence of opportunistic behavior by employers takes the form of specific court cases, two of which are discussed here. In both instances, the presence of a pension increased the risk of layoff.

DeSoto, Inc.

Four former employees of DeSoto have charged that in 1989 the company laid off 10 percent of its workforce in an effort to increase the overfunding in its pension plan and thereby help avert a takeover attempt.[3] The laid-off employees filed suit in U.S. District Court in Chicago to stop the company from terminating its pension plan and from distributing $28 million in after-tax surplus assets to its shareholders. The plaintiffs, who had each worked at the company for between 16 and 29 years, argued that DeSoto had laid off 200 employees late in 1989 as part of an effort to thwart a $50-per-share hostile takeover bid by Sutton Holding Corporation of New York. As of late 1992, this case had not been decided.

Continental Can Company

The U.S. Court of Appeals for the Third Circuit ruled that a nationwide program at Continental Can Company targeted for layoff those employees who were approaching pension eligibility and thus violated the terms of ERISA.[4] This upheld a district court judge's injunction against the use of the plan (*McLendon v. Continental Can Co.*, CA 3, No. 89-5596, 7/26/90).

Under a 1977 collective bargaining agreement with the United Steel Workers, Continental established "magic number" pension benefits to ensure benefits for employees subjected to periodic (temporary) layoffs. Benefits under the plan, which accrued when the employee reached a certain age and a certain number of years of service, included layoff benefits to those employees experiencing a break-in-service of two years or more from plant shutdowns, involuntary layoffs, or physical disability.

Faced with both substantial unfunded liabilities under the pension plan and a dwindling market for steel beverage cans, Continental Can devised the "bell system," a nationwide program subsequently found by a federal judge to stand as a reverse acronym for "Let's Limit Employee Benefits" or "Lowest Level of Employee Benefits." A computer program generated printouts of the workforce with codes attached to each worker showing benefit eligibility and identifying which employees were close to vesting.

Four employees who lost their jobs brought a class action against the company in 1983, charging that Continental had implemented the "bell system" to avoid pension liabilities in violation of section 510 of ERISA. The plaintiffs maintained that they were laid off because they were approaching eligibility for magic number pension benefits, and that Continental kept them on permanent layoff, even when jobs were available, to prevent them from achieving a vested right to benefits.

The company claimed that the system was strictly informational and that the employees who were laid off lost their jobs because of the industry slowdown. In 1989, Judge H. Lee Sarokin of the U.S. District Court in New Jersey found that Continental had "engaged in a complex, secret and deliberate scheme to deny its workers bargained-for pensions (that) raises questions of corporate morality, ethics and decency which far transcend the factual and legal issues posed by this matter." After several appeals, Continental Can agreed to a $45 million settlement as a final resolution of the case.

Evidence of Pensions Associated with Fewer Layoffs

These court cases appear to be isolated examples of situations in which the presence of a pension increased the likelihood of layoffs. Virtually all economic studies that examine the more general experience conclude the opposite: workers who are covered by a pension are less likely to be laid off than workers who are not covered.

Several studies have examined both quits and layoffs (i.e., Mitchell 1982; Allen, Clark, and McDermed 1986; Even and Macpherson 1990a). In general, these studies find that the relationship between pensions and worker mobility is even more negative for total job change than for quits.[5] Only a few studies explicitly examine the impact of pensions on layoffs (Parnes, Gagen, and King 1981; Cornwell, Dorsey, and Mehrzad 1991; Allen, Clark, and McDermed 1990).

Parnes, Gagen, and King (1981) investigate whether the presence of a pension affects the likelihood of being permanently laid off. Using the National Longitudinal Survey of Mature Men, they identify men who at the time of the initial (1966) survey had been with their current employer for at least five years and who were permanently separated from that employer sometime between 1966 and 1975. Because their concern is with displaced workers for whom layoffs are unaccustomed events, Parnes, Gagen, and King exclude workers in construction and agriculture. According to their multiple classification analysis, older male workers with pensions are considerably less likely to be displaced than older male workers without pensions: the likelihood of displacement is approximately 5 percent for men with pensions and 12 percent for men without pensions.

Cornwell, Dorsey, and Mehrzad (1991) also use the National Longitudinal Survey of Mature Men; however, they select men who were discharged between 1971 and 1976 and do not exclude workers in construction and agriculture. (They do, however, exclude self-employed workers.) Despite these differences, their results are similar to those of Parnes, Gagen, and King. They find that, on average, the likelihood that an older pension-covered worker will be laid off is 4.6 to 5.4 percentage points lower than that for an older, noncovered worker.[6]

In addition, Cornwell, Dorsey, and Mehrzad examine whether the value of potential pension loss affects dismissals among older male workers. Their results on this are mixed. When the pension loss calculations are based on a constant wage-pension tradeoff, the pension loss coefficient is zero and is insignificant.[7] Coupled with the negative and significant coefficient on the pension coverage variable, this signifies that while workers with pensions are less likely to be discharged, the risk among covered workers is no higher for workers with greater potential losses. However, when the pension loss calculations ignore the wage-pension tradeoff, the pension loss coefficient becomes larger and significant, signifying that a higher loss raises the risk of layoff.

The Cornwell, Dorsey, and Mehrzad study tests whether firms behave in an opportunistic manner. Although the authors find no empirical support for the idea that pensions raise the risk of layoff for older male workers, they point out that, because the agreed-upon risk of discharge will probably be lower for pension-covered workers in an implicit contract, their findings do not necessarily rule out opportunistic behavior. As a further examination of the issue of opportunistic behavior, they investigate whether unanticipated pension losses increase the likelihood of layoffs. They find that workers with greater unexpected losses are more likely to be discharged. They also attempt to test whether firms with declining profits and declining reputation capital are more likely to behave in an opportunistic manner, but their results are insignificant. Their final test is an examination of the effect of ERISA on the probability of dismissal. They cannot reject the hypothesis that ERISA had no effect on the propensity of employers to dismiss workers who were covered by pensions.

Like Cornwell, Dorsey, and Mehrzad (1991), Allen, Clark, and McDermed (1990) explore whether pension losses affect layoffs. However, because they use the Panel Study of Income Dynamics (PSID) rather than the National Longitudinal Survey of Mature Men, they look at all workers rather than just older male workers. Their PSID sample, which covers the period 1975-82, consists of private wage and salary workers who were employed at the time of the 1975 survey and reported earnings. They selected only those workers under age 55 (in 1975) who were heads of household working 35 or more hours per week, and they excluded individuals employed in agriculture, forestry, fishing, and unclassified trade industries. Allen, Clark, and McDermed find that for these workers the probability of being laid off falls by 1.3 percent for each $1,000 increase in the capital loss of the pension.[8] (Recall that this is not consistent with the findings of Cornwell, Dorsey, and Mehrzad, who find a positive relationship between the two.)[9] The capital loss has a much larger effect on layoffs than on quits. Allen, Clark, and McDermed do not explain why there is a smaller impact on quits, but they point out that the observed negative relationship between layoffs and capital loss is consistent with models that portray pensions as "part of an implicit contract where bonding prevents shirking and reputational concerns prevent employers from pocketing...(*the capital loss*)...by firing their workers" (Allen, Clark, and McDermed 1990, p. 26).

In summary, econometric studies on the relationship between pensions and layoffs suggest that the presence of a pension is associated with fewer layoffs. However, the evidence on the relationship between pension loss and the probability of layoff is mixed. In general, the research findings are consistent with models that view pensions as part of an implicit contract between workers and firms. Although none of the findings rules out opportunistic behavior by firms, they suggest that opportunism does not dominate.

Researchers have not yet fully explored the reasons why these empirical studies indicate a negative relationship between pension coverage and layoffs. This remains fertile ground for future research.

THE IMPACT OF LAYOFFS ON PENSION BENEFITS

Pension-covered workers who are laid off can suffer the same portability losses as workers who quit their jobs. However, laid-off workers may incur additional losses as well. These losses are associated with the inability of many displaced workers to find jobs equivalent to the ones from which they were laid off (i.e., their new job may offer a lower wage or a less generous pension or no pension at all). In addition, laid-off workers may decide to drop out of the labor force because the job prospects are so bleak, or they may experience lengthy periods of unemployment. Some displaced workers may receive benefits (i.e., severance pay) to help compensate them for their losses. However, in many cases, these benefits fail to compensate them for lost earnings, let alone pension benefit loses.

Although laid-off workers do not inevitably find themselves in these situation, one of the empirical regularities that distinguishes quits from layoffs is that laid-off workers are far more likely to encounter these adversities than workers who quit. Policymakers who are concerned with the impact of turnover on pension benefit loss should be aware of these potential situations and take them into account when designing policy.

Nonportability Losses

In addition to portability losses, workers who are laid off may incur other pension losses based on their subsequent employment experience.

Losses from Lower Wages or Less Generous Pension

Reemployed displaced workers may suffer pension benefit losses either because their new job offers a pension with less generous terms or because their reemployment wage (and subsequent earnings path) is lower than what it otherwise would have been. There is no evidence on the likelihood that a laid-off worker will be reemployed in a job offering a pension with less generous terms. However, there is a considerable amount of research on the impact of layoffs on reemployment wages which affect the pension benefits of covered workers.

In summarizing the literature on wage loss associated with layoffs, Hamermesh (1989) states that, on average, reemployment wages are 5 to 15 percent below wages on the terminated job. Gustman and Steinmeier (1990) present evidence that pension-covered jobs may be at the high end of this range. Using data from the 1984-87 PSID for males age 31 to 50, they estimate that the mean wage of involuntary movers from pension-covered jobs falls by 9.1 percent, while the wage of involuntary movers from non-pension-covered jobs rises by 4.1 percent.[10]

Examining the average wage loss associated with layoffs obscures the substantial variation in what happens to workers when they are laid off. Each of the three Displaced Worker Surveys shows that about half of the displaced workers earn as much or more in their new job as they did in the job from which they were terminated. However, approximately 30 percent of the workers earn 20 percent or more less (Flaim and Sehgal 1985; Horvath 1987; Herz 1990). If this decline in wages persists over time, the pension-covered workers in this group will suffer moderate benefit losses (assuming benefits are based on earnings).

Losses from having No Pension

Some displaced workers find themselves without a pension after they are laid off. This can occur for two reasons. Either the new job does not offer a pension, or the worker remains unemployed and may permanently drop out of the labor force. Only a small percentage of workers who were laid off permanently drop out of the labor force. Information on the dropout rate is limited, but using the longitudinal capabilities of the CPS, Devens (1986) provides evidence that less than 15 percent of displaced workers remain permanently out of the labor force. Those workers who were covered by a pension may suffer considerable loss of benefits.

Similarly, pension-covered displaced workers who are reemployed in jobs that do not offer pensions may also suffer losses. There are several reasons why laid-off workers may be reemployed in nonpension jobs. First, some workers may decide to take part-time jobs, which are less likely to offer a pension than full-time jobs. According to the first and second Displaced Worker Surveys, of the displaced workers with three or more years of tenure who worked full time on their terminated job and who were able to find new jobs after being laid off, approximately 10 to 12 percent were in part-time jobs. Another 8 percent were self-employed, and the remainder were in full-time wage and salary jobs (Flaim and Sehgal 1985; Horvath 1987).[11] A second reason is that some laid-off workers, particularly those who lose jobs in declining industries, must switch industries in order to find a new job. As shown in table 11.1, the general tendency is for workers to move from jobs in the goods-producing industries (especially manufacturing), where pension coverage is high, to jobs in the services and trade industries, where pension coverage is low. For example, only 39.8 percent of the (reemployed) workers who were displaced from jobs in durable goods manufacturing were reemployed in that industry. Almost 17 percent went into wholesale and retail trade, where pension coverage rates were considerably lower. Another 16 percent went into services.

Gustman and Steinmeier (1990, tables A1 and A4) present wide-ranging evidence on the extent to which pension-covered displaced workers are reemployed in jobs that do not offer pensions. Using panel data from the 1983-86 Survey of Consumer Finances (SCF) for males 31-50 years old, they find that 48 percent of involuntary movers who had a pension on their terminated job did not have a pension on their new job. Their data from the 1984-85 Survey of Income and Program Participation (SIPP), which also covers males 31-50 years old, show a much higher percentage: 71 percent of involuntary movers who had a pension on their initial job did not have a pension on their new job. There are several possible reasons for these varying estimates, including small sample sizes and problems with both the SCF and SIPP data (discussed in Gustman and Steinmeier 1990).[12]

Hutchens (1986) also presents evidence relevant to this issue. He finds that firms offering pensions are less likely to hire older workers

Table 11.1

Reemployed Workers by Industry of Lost Job and Industry of Job Held in January 1984
and Pension Coverage Rates by Industry, 1983

Industry of lost job	Total (000s)	Construction	Percentage distribution by industry in January 1984			Transportation & public utilities	Wholesale & retail trade	Services	Other	Pension coverage rates 1983
			Manufacturing							
			Total	Durable goods	Nondurable goods					
Total	3,058	10.6	28.3	18.7	9.6	7.5	20.7	21.0	11.8	47
Construction	281	43.6	6.2	4.0	2.2	4.2	12.6	23.2	10.3	32
Manufacturing	1,474	7.4	47.1	31.1	15.8	5.0	15.4	16.8	8.4	NA
Durable goods	980	8.5	46.1	39.8	6.3	5.4	16.7	15.6	7.8	67
Nondurable goods	493	5.1	48.6	14.0	34.7	4.4	12.9	19.3	9.7	59
Transportation & public utilities	198	11.6	12.3	7.7	4.6	42.6	11.8	11.5	10.2	53 (T) 81 (PU)
Wholesale & retail trade	455	4.1	14.6	9.0	5.6	5.4	50.1	16.8	8.9	47 (WT)
Services	347	7.6	12.0	8.1	3.9	3.6	19.4	46.4	10.9	35
Other	300	8.7	7.4	5.0	2.3	6.3	17.7	23.5	36.4	

SOURCE: Beller and Lawrence (1992).

(over age 55). Thus, older workers laid off from a pension job are probably less likely to find another pension job than are younger laid-off workers.

Income Replacement for Laid-Off Workers

Laid-off workers may receive compensation from a variety of federal, state, and private sources. These include unemployment insurance, supplemental unemployment insurance, severance pay, trade adjustment assistance, plant closing benefits, and pension-vesting credit for an extra year of service. There are two reasons why compensation is important to consider *vis a vis* pension benefit losses. First, if the compensation either partially or fully offsets the pension losses, then the losses incurred by laid-off workers may not be an especially important policy issue. The policy debate can focus generally on the impact of turnover on pension benefit losses without taking the laid-off workers explicitly into account.

The existence of compensation for laid-off workers provides a test of implicit contract theory. Dorsey (1990) points out that the portability losses incurred by workers who quit act as a penalty to these workers for breaking an implicit long-term contract with their employers. However, workers who are laid off also suffer these portability losses. Dorsey argues that, in the case of layoffs, firms are breaking the implicit contract, and there should therefore be a penalty to the firm (if indeed implicit contract theory accurately describes the employer-employee relationship). If the firm pays laid-off workers directly (e.g., through severance pay) or indirectly (e.g., through contributions to an unemployment insurance fund), then this can represent a partial penalty to the firm. In both cases, the magnitude of compensation relative to the wage and pension losses is of interest.

The three Displaced Worker Surveys, which feature the most complete set of information on laid-off workers, include questions on unemployment insurance only. These data suggest that a considerable number of displaced workers fail to receive enough benefits to cover their lost earnings, let alone their pension losses. According to these surveys, about half of the laid-off workers who received unemployment insurance had exhausted their benefits by the time of the survey (Flaim and Sehgal 1985; Horvath 1987; Herz 1990).

This conclusion is supported by findings from a 1983-84 survey of 379 workers who were put on indefinite layoff by a major automobile manufacturer in April 1983 (cited in Flaim and Sehgal 1985, p. 14). This survey found that, on average, compensation payments covered about 30 percent of the displaced workers' income loss. The amount of income offset by these benefits was lower the longer the layoff period. The benefits covered about 55 percent of lost income for workers laid off for less than one year; however, they covered only 13 percent for workers laid off for more than two years. The proportion of lost income offset by the compensation payments also varied with seniority. The benefits received by workers with more than 10 years of seniority replaced a larger proportion of lost income than those received by workers with less seniority.

Thus, there is some limited evidence that for some workers compensation benefits fail to offset lost income. However, there is other evidence that this is not the case for all laid-off workers. Flaim and Sehgal (1985, p. 14) cite the following finding from a demonstration study (conducted in the early 1980s) involving laid-off automobile workers from the Detroit metropolitan area:

> Depending upon the particular plant from which they had been laid off, the workers were found to have received either unemployment insurance benefits, or unemployment insurance coupled with company-funded supplemental unemployment benefits, or, in some cases, both of these benefits as well as trade adjustment assistance, which was paid to those whose jobs were deemed to have been lost because of imports. Therefore, some of the workers had their pre-layoff earnings almost entirely replaced by benefits, at least for a time.

Moreover, there is some indication that under certain circumstances some severance plans can compensate laid-off workers for more than just lost earnings. For example, some severance plans are structured so that, regardless of how long it takes to find a new job, an eligible laid-off employee receives a certain number of weeks of salary based on years of service.[13] Under this type of plan, a worker who is laid off after 10 years of service may receive 10 weeks of severance pay (at the rate of pay before termination). If the worker finds a new job after two weeks and if the new job features at least the same rate of pay as the old job, then the worker will receive eight weeks of compensation in excess of lost earnings. This could offset some of the worker's loss in pension wealth. Other severance plans stop payments when the worker begins a new job. However, some of these plans offer laid-off workers a guaranteed minimum, i.e., if the employee is entitled to a maximum of 18 weeks of severance pay but finds a job within three weeks, that employee receives the guaranteed minimum, say 13 weeks of severance pay. Again, in cases like this, certain laid-off employees may receive more than their lost earnings, and thus be compensated for some of their loss of pension wealth.

It is not known how common these particular types of severance plans are. In general, however, severance plans are fairly common. The most recent Employee Benefits Survey shows that 39 percent of all full-time employees in medium-size and large firms (defined as employing at least 100 workers) were eligible for severance pay (U.S. Department of Labor 1990). The percentage is higher for professional and administrative employees (54 percent) and technical and clerical workers (46 percent) than for production and service employees (27 percent).[14] These figures are similar to those from a U.S. Government Accounting Office (1986) survey conducted in the mid-1980s. This survey covered firms that appeared to have laid off workers recently and found that 54 percent of these firms offered severance pay. The percentages were higher for white-collar workers (53 percent) than for blue-collar workers (34 percent).[15] Doescher and Dorsey (1992) found that explicit pension plan provisions for early retirement bonuses in the event of a major layoff are common. Allowing older workers to begin receiving benefits immediately reduces or eliminates their pension losses. They also found that severance pay plans were more likely in firms that also sponsored defined benefit pensions. This result is consistent with the prediction that employers will attempt to offset defined benefit pension losses of job losers. Clearly, further research is needed to identify the extent to which benefits paid to laid-off workers compensate them for lost earnings and lost pension wealth. At issue is whether these benefits in any way offset the pension wealth losses incurred by workers when they are laid off.

Policy Implications of Layoffs

The effect of layoffs on pension benefit losses is an important policy issue, not because it affects a large number of workers, but because it is such an important issue for those it does affect. To date, most of the policy focus has been on preserving the pension benefits of mobile workers in general, with little distinction between workers who quit and those who are laid off. This section first discusses how the general policy proposals will affect laid-off workers. It then suggests the kinds of policies that could help the small minority of high-tenure workers who suffer serious pension losses when they are laid off.

In general, the policies directed at preserving the pension benefits of mobile workers can be classified as either policies that affect the portability of pensions or policies explicitly designed to preserve retirement income. While these policies may meet most of the needs of workers who voluntarily quit their jobs, they only address some of the concerns of workers who are involuntarily laid off. The policies designed to enhance portability generally focus on plan design changes. Some proposals call for more liberal vesting requirements, while others attempt to expand service portability.

Requiring shorter vesting schedules would enhance portability by allowing more short-tenure workers to carry accrued pension benefits with them when they change jobs. About 70 percent of all laid-off workers had less than five years of tenure. While not all of these workers are covered by pension plans, this statistic suggests that a high percentage of displaced workers lose their pension benefits because they are not vested. Policies to tighten vesting requirements will reduce the number of short-tenure workers who must forfeit their accrued benefits when they are laid off.

Policies designed to enhance service portability will also help displaced workers. A vested worker who is covered by a defined benefit plan and is laid off will suffer a pension benefit loss due to backloading. Policies requiring either that the vested benefits of separated participants be adjusted for inflation or the defined benefit plans give participants credit for service at previous jobs or that permit only defined contribution plans would help blunt this loss. A policy that requires indexing would eliminate most of the loss from backloading, as would a policy that permits only defined contribution plans. How-

ever, policies that call for pooling of service credits or require employers to credit all years of service in the workforce would only be
effective for workers who are reemployed in jobs that offer pension
coverage. Because the general tendency is for laid-off workers to leave
jobs in industries where pension coverage is high for jobs in industries
where pension coverage is lower (table 11.1), these types of policies
could seriously undermine elimination of losses due to backloading for
laid-off workers.

While the portability policies discussed above will help laid-off
workers, it is not clear that the policies designed to preserve retirement
income will do so. The primary focus of policies designed to preserve
retirement income is to limit the use of lump-sum distributions for current consumption. This involves placing limits on preretirement distributions, increasing the tax penalties on distributions that are not rolled
over, and simplifying the transfer of distributions into qualified retirement accounts. As is the case for workers in general, these types of policies will help preserve retirement income for laid-off workers.
However, some displaced workers may be better off if they can use
their accrued pension benefits to help them through a lengthy period of
unemployment. Policies permitting hardship distributions would be
one way to help displaced workers.

It is important to note that neither the portability policies nor the
preservation-of-retirement-income policies address some of the more
significant pension benefit losses incurred by some displaced workers,
in particular losses associated with failure to find a new job or with taking a new job that does not offer a pension. These losses must be
addressed through other channels.[16] One way to do this might be to
require that pension plans offer laid-off workers some kind of nonmon-
etary bonus or credit to compensate them for their loss. For example,
some pension plans automatically vest laid-off workers. Others credit
laid-off workers with an extra year of service for vesting purposes
(Pension Rights Center 1990-1991). Requiring plans to include either
of these provisions, or a similar provision (e.g., offering laid-off workers an extra year of service for purposes of computing benefits), could
help compensate displaced workers for their loss in pension wealth.

Another approach might be to directly compensate workers for their
pension losses. This could occur through any of the programs currently
in place to compensate displaced workers for their lost earnings. For

example, the trade adjustment assistance program and perhaps the unemployment insurance program could be expanded to cover compensation for lost pension wealth. Similarly, severance payments and plant-closing benefits could be structured so that they include pension wealth compensation for laid-off workers.

Any serious consideration of these proposals should include an assessment of costs. It is also important to determine to what extent laid-off workers are currently compensated for their wage and pension losses. The current literature offers only scant information on this point.

CONCLUSIONS

Both workers who quit and workers who are laid off can incur several different types of losses. Portability policies will help with the vesting losses and backloading losses incurred by workers experiencing both types of turnover; preservation-of-retirement-income policies, on the other hand, will help workers who quit, but may make displaced workers worse off. The other categories of pension wealth loss—losses incurred because of either a less generous pension on the new job or no pension at all following the layoff—will not be addressed by current proposals to enhance portability and preserve retirement income. For workers who quit, this is not a major concern because they voluntarily incur the pension losses. For laid-off workers, however, it is important to know the extent to which the benefits paid compensate them for lost earnings and lost pension wealth. If the benefits either fully or partially offset the pension wealth losses, then policies designed to enhance pension portability may be sufficient to meet the needs of laid-off workers. However, if the benefits do not offset their losses, then there may be a need to develop special policies for workers who incur losses in their pension wealth due to being laid off.

NOTES

1. This chapter was written by Tabitha Doescher.

2. Firms that engage in this type of deceptive behavior may have considerable difficulties recruiting a quality workforce. Further, some aspects of this type of behavior would violate federal pension law.

3. This case was reported in Chernoff (1990, pp. 2, 38).

4. This case was reported in Bureau of National Affairs (1990).

5. Although this finding seems to suggest that pensions deter layoffs even more than they deter quits, the results are sometimes confounded by the inclusion of temporary layoffs in total job changes.

6. This may include temporary, as well as permanent, layoffs.

7. In this regression, the pension loss calculations assume that workers receive a pension in lieu of higher wages. Thus, the pension loss calculations net out the sacrifice of future wages. The tradeoff is assumed to be a constant fraction of the wage.

8. This may include temporary, as well as permanent, layoffs.

9. Cornwell, Dorsey, and Mehrzad obtained their pension loss data from Robert Clark, so the difference between the two studies cannot be attributed to differences in calculating the pension loss (or capital loss) variable. One possible explanation is that Cornwell, Dorsey, and Mehrzad look at older male workers only, whereas Allen, Clark, and McDermed examine workers who were under age 55 at the beginning of the study.

10. These figures from both Hamermesh and Gustman and Steinmeier are simply comparisons between the real wage at the time of the layoff and the real reemployment wage; they do not take into account any merit or productivity wage increases which may have occurred in the absence of displacement. For those workers with lengthy periods of unemployment, this could be a sizable omission.

11. These surveys were conducted during downturns in the economy. The statistics may vary over the business cycle.

12. It is interesting to contrast these data with information on the current pension status of workers who participated in a pension plan on a prior job. Using the May 1988 CPS, Piacentini (1990a, table 2) reports that 69 percent of private-sector, full- time workers who participated in a pension plan on a prior job were covered by a pension on their current job; 53 percent reported that they were currently participating in a plan. These figures were 70 percent and 56 percent, respectively, for the males in the sample (tabulations for males ages 31-50, the group used by Gustman and Steinmeier, were not available). Thus, 30 percent of the males who had a pension on a previous job were not covered by a pension on their current job, while 44 percent were not currently participating in a pension plan. (Note that these data include males who quit their previous job, as well as those who were laid off.) This is only a slightly lower percentage than that found by Gustman and Steinmeier for laid-off males included in the Survey of Consumer Finances; however, it is a considerably higher percentage than that found in the Survey of Income and Program Participation.

13. With this type of plan, there is no built-in disincentive to avoid job search.

14. The Employee Benefits Survey also contains information on supplemental unemployment benefits, which are much less common than severance plans. Five percent of all full-time employees are eligible for supplemental unemployment benefits. The percentage is higher for production and service employees (9 percent) than for professional and administrative employees and technical and clerical workers (2 percent each).

15. The General Accounting Office survey also shows that 16 percent of the firms offered early retirement to laid-off workers, 15 percent offered pay in lieu of notice, 10 percent offered

lump-sum payments, 10 percent offered supplementary unemployment benefits, 43 percent offered continuation of health insurance, and 28 percent offered continuation of life insurance. Except for supplementary unemployment benefits, the white-collar percentages were higher than the blue-collar percentages.

16. These losses may also be incurred by workers who quit their jobs. However, workers who quit are presumably doing so voluntarily. There is no perceived policy need to compensate them for these losses. Laid-off workers are a different matter. Because these workers leave their jobs involuntarily, it may be desirable to provide them with some kind of compensation.

12

An International Perspective on Pension Portability

In searching for solutions to the pension portability problem, policy analysts should consider all available evidence on the range and feasibility of policies. Because several countries have done more than the United States to reduce pension benefit loss, a close look at their policies might answer a number of feasibility questions faced by U.S. policymakers.[1]

This chapter examines portability policies in countries with private pension systems similar to those of the United States and focuses on policy aspects that may be applicable to the U.S. pension system.[2] The countries considered are Canada, Japan, the Netherlands, and the United Kingdom. Each has a well-developed private pension system where employers voluntarily provide pension benefits. Other western industrialized countries, such as Germany, France, and Italy, have pension systems that differ considerably from those of the United States, and for that reason they are considered in less detail.

BACKGROUND

Employer-sponsored private pension systems in Japan, the Netherlands, the United Kingdom, and the United States are regulated by the national government. In contrast, pensions in Canada are regulated by the provincial governments, with each province having separate standards for its pension plans.[3]

The province of Ontario employs 40 percent of Canada's private-sector workers and thus represents a major part of the country's experience. Ontario has been a leader in pension reform, with other provinces often copying its policies. For this reason, Ontario is treated as representing Canadian pension policy for purposes of this chapter.

Employer-sponsored pensions in the Netherlands are nearly universal for full-time workers. By contrast, less than half of the private-sector labor force in the United States, Canada, Japan, and the United Kingdom is covered by an employer-sponsored pension plan. The three English-speaking countries, however, all provide tax advantages for individual retirement accounts, which can substitute for employer-sponsored pensions. Workers may use IRAs for pension portability, since they can transfer preretirement distributions from employer-sponsored pensions to an individual account. Workers also may choose an individual plan as a portable alternative to an employer-sponsored pension. While individual plans are not available in Japan, until recently Japanese workers could have tax free savings accounts, which could be used like an IRA.

Patterns of job change vary across countries (table 12.1), possibly reflecting the differing attitudes towards job change. Only 4 percent of Japanese workers left their jobs over a one-year period (Yumiba 1991), while 11 percent of British workers did so (Daykin 1991). In the Netherlands and the United States, 7 percent of workers changed jobs in a year (Keizer 1991). In all four countries, women more commonly changed jobs than men (table 12.1). In Japan and the United Kingdom, young males more commonly changed jobs than older males (table 12.2).

Table 12.1
Job Changers as a Percentage of Labor Force

	Total	Males	Females
Japan	4.2	3.8	4.8
Netherlands	6.7	6.5	7.3
United Kingdom	11.0	10.0	14.0
United States	6.5	NA	NA

SOURCE: Turner and Dailey (1991).

Canada, Japan, and the United Kingdom have a two-tiered social security system. The first tier provides a flat benefit per person, and the second tier provides an earnings-related benefit. Japan and the United Kingdom allow workers to "contract out" of the earnings-related part of social security. Employers can cut social security payments if they fund equivalent pensions, and the contracted-out pension plans have all of the portability features of social security. British workers also can opt out of the earnings-related part of social security (the State Earnings Related Pension) by contributing to an individual Personal Pension Plan. But it is only financially beneficial for workers under the ages of 40 to 45 to do so because of the long period needed to accumulate sufficient benefits in a Personal Pension Plan. Non-contracted-out pensions are the ones that correspond most closely to U.S. private pensions.

In Canada, the Netherlands, and the United Kingdom, defined benefit plans are often contributory—workers and employers both contribute to the plan. This creates portability problems not faced in the United States, where contributory defined benefit plans are rare. In Japan and the Netherlands almost all plans are defined benefit plans. Canada and the United Kingdom have some defined contribution plans, but they are not as common as in the United States. Thus, while the United States does not have some portability features provided in other countries, portability features of U.S. defined contribution plans generally are not found elsewhere.

Table 12.2
Percentage of Males Who Changed Jobs as a Percentage
of All Male Employees by Age, 1987 and 1989

Age range	United Kingdom (1987)	Japan (1989)
<25	21.6	11.0
25-34	12.0	4.8
35-44	7.0	2.6
45-54 }	4.0	2.0
55-59 }	4.0	3.1
60-64	2.0	
65>	NA	1.7

SOURCE: Turner and Dailey (1991).

Most Japanese pension plans are severance pay plans, yielding lump sum benefits whenever employment ends, whether at retirement age or earlier. Vested deferred benefits for job leavers are not maintained with the former employer.

PORTABILITY POLICIES

The following section focuses on particular portability policies that have been adopted in other countries, comparing vesting standards, preretirement indexing, service portability, and lump sum distribution. Because the Netherlands is the only European country where a new employer bears liability for a worker's pensionable service with a prior employer, the manner in which the Dutch handle service portability is examined in depth.

Vesting Standards

The maximum period for a Dutch, British, or Canadian worker to vest is less than for an American. In the Netherlands, workers must vest after participating one year in a plan, though participation may be restricted until age 25 or later. The United Kingdom requires vesting after two years of participation, but workers are usually eligible to participate at age 19 after one year of work. Ontario requires vesting after two years of tenure in a plan.

Japan is the only one of these countries with no legislated vesting rules, yet Japanese pension plans provide rapid vesting even without regulations.[4] Less than 15 percent of workers are in plans that require over two years if separation is initiated by the employer. By contrast, 60 percent of workers are in plans that require over two years if separation is voluntary. Even for long service, the firm pays higher lump sums if the firm rather than the worker ends the job.

Vesting is immediate in France, but it requires 10 years of service and age 35, or 12 years of service, in Germany. In Denmark contributions vest, but benefits do not.[5]

Preretirement Indexing

When a worker changes jobs and the plan indexes deferred benefits for inflation, the employer pays for much of the portability loss that otherwise occurs with job change. In the Netherlands, most plans voluntarily index deferred vested benefits. Also in the Netherlands, if the plan awards benefit increases or cost-of-living adjustments to its retirees, it must grant the same increases to former workers with deferred pensions.

British law requires plans to inflation-index deferred vested benefits. Legislation requires plans to index benefits before retirement for job leavers, up to 5 percent annually based on increases in retail prices. Ireland, starting in 1996, will require plans to index deferred vested benefits up to 4 percent annually. Because of the caps, these systems completely index benefits only if inflation is low.[6] Plans are not required to index deferred vested benefits in Canada or the United States and rarely do so.

Japanese plans do not index deferred vested benefits because job leavers receive accrued benefits as a lump sum payment at separation. Japan has considered lifetime employment with one employer as the most desirable career pattern; thus policymakers have had little concern for minimizing portability losses.

Portability of Service

Plans transfer deferred vested benefits in the Netherlands through five portability clearinghouses called transfer circuits. A plan may participate in a portability clearinghouse, and most large pension plans do. The private sector set up clearinghouses in 1987 after the Dutch government indicated that it would mandate a solution if the private sector did not develop a way to eliminate pension benefit losses for job leavers.

The clearinghouses require plans to use benefit formulas based on final average salary and years worked and allow insured and noninsured plans to participate. In 1988, 78 percent of workers (including government employees) in a pension plan were in a plan belonging to a portability clearinghouse (Keizer 1991). A job leaver may leave the vested rights in a former employer's pension plan or use a clearinghouse to transfer them to a new employer's plan.

Small pension plans in the Netherlands provide portability in a different manner. Most are insured through purchase of individual policies under a group arrangement and may transfer the paid-up policy to job leavers.

A Dutch worker who leaves a job has a right to a deferred pension in proportion to his/her service relative to a full career. Before the mid 1980s, the worker only had a right to a deferred pension based on the paid-up premiums (for an insured plan). The funding methods used often made the former sum much less than the pension figured in proportion to service.

Key to reducing portability losses through an employer-based system is deciding who pays for the losses—the former employer or the new employer. This issue is complicated when plans use different actuarial assumptions. The interest rate and wage growth rate assumptions strongly affect the calculated value of pension liabilities. The gap between these two assumptions is key in figuring whether the old or new employer pays the extra sum needed to cut the portability loss.

Usually the interest rate assumption is 1 or 2 percentage points higher than the wage growth rate assumption for figuring liabilities in an ongoing plan. The more the interest rate assumption exceeds the wage growth rate assumption the less the sum transferred by the former employer. With a difference between the two assumptions of 1 or 2 percentage points for figuring a job leaver's liability, the former employer would pay for the portability loss otherwise occurring. That pattern of assumptions is equivalent to projecting wages and using a market interest rate.

In the Netherlands, to figure the sum transferred by the former employer to the clearinghouse, uniform actuarial assumptions must be used. These assumptions exclude decrements to pension liabilities other than mortality (no job turnover assumed) and future salary increases (a zero wage growth rate assumption), and include a 4 percent interest rate for discounting future liabilities. With a 4 percent interest rate assumption and a zero wage growth assumption, the old employer transfers more assets than had he/she assumed a market interest rate, say 7 percent, and a zero wage growth assumption. Future liabilities are discounted at a lower real rate in the first instance. With these assumptions, the former employer pays for some future benefits arising due to the effect on benefits of future wage growth credited to past service.

When figuring asset transfer value in the Netherlands, however, the accrued liability's present value derived by using these assumptions is further cut. It is reduced by a percentage depending on the difference between the 4 percent interest rate and the interest rate on a portfolio of government bonds. The cut is not sufficiently large to make the liability equivalent to that figured using a zero wage growth rate assumption and a market interest rate.

These adjustments produce a liability causing the former employer to pay for part of the effect of future salary increases on the benefit for the transferred service. The new employer, however, must pay a large part of the effect of future wage growth on past service.[7] The Netherlands is the only European Community country where the new employer has a liability for the effect of future wage growth on pensionable service with a prior employer. In all other countries, the worker loses this advantage.

Japan has two portability clearinghouses—one that handles large plans and one that is dedicated to smaller groups. Until 1989, the clearinghouse for large plans—run by the government Pension Fund Association—only accepted transfers of pensions up to the sum contracted out of social security. Since 1989, it has accepted the contracted-out portion of a pension as well as any additional pension benefit. The clearinghouse for small plans—Smaller Enterprise Retirement Allowances Mutual Aid Plans—is used by only 3 percent of eligible job leavers.

In the United Kingdom some nationalized British industries operate "transfer clubs," where uniform actuarial factors determine the accrued vested benefit to which a worker is entitled. The receiving plan grants added years of service using the same factors; however, few employers have taken advantage of these arrangements (Atkins 1991).

A British worker changing jobs may transfer his/her benefit to an approved individual insurance policy. The benefit value must be figured using a current long-term interest rate. The calculation need not consider future pay raises, but must consider statutory preretirement inflation indexing.

One of the more bureaucratically efficient pension portability systems is found in Israel, where most workers are covered under a single pension plan sponsored by the major labor union. Thus, when workers change jobs, they lose no benefits because they do not change pension plans.

Lump Sum Distributions

In contrast to Canada, the Netherlands, and the United Kingdom, workers in Japan normally receive a lump sum payment of accrued benefits when they change jobs. (Lump sum payment is also the normal benefit payment at retirement.) Because Japanese savings rates have been high, Japanese policymakers have not been concerned that preretirement distributions would be used for nonretirement purposes. Their lack of concern contrasts with the concern of U.S. policymakers that workers save too little for retirement when allowed to spend retirement savings.

In Ontario, vested pension benefits cannot be received in a preretirement lump sum distribution. They must be locked in and can only be received as a lifetime annuity paid during retirement.[8] The only lump sum distributions permitted are for disabled persons, pensions below a stipulated value, and 25 percent of the value of deferred pensions accrued pre-1987. In cases where benefits are only plan-vested and not statutorily vested (the plan has more rapid vesting than law requires), such sums may be refunded if the plan allows. If a worker has contributed to a pension plan but has not worked long enough to vest, the contributions plus interest are returned to the worker when he/she changes jobs.

In Canada, transfers of assets can be made to a Registered Retirement Savings Plan (RRSP), which is like an American IRA. The assets in an RRSP, however, are locked in with no possibility of withdrawal until retirement age. In theory, assets can be transferred to a new employer's plan, but most employers will not accept such assets. If the plan rules specify, the deferred pension's present value can also be used to purchase a life annuity from an insurance company; however, the annuity must not begin before the worker is eligible for early retirement. A divorced spouse with an order for spousal benefits under the Family Law Act of 1986 must have the same benefit options as the participant.

The Netherlands permits preretirement lump sum distributions only of the worker's contributions before vesting, transfer of funds to another plan, or emigration.

In the United Kingdom only unvested contributions can be returned to the participant who is changing jobs; all other benefits are locked in.[9] Thus, after two years in a plan, workers cannot receive preretirement distributions. Recent legislation, however, gives job leavers options for transferring funds. Preretirement distributions may be moved to another plan, placed in a Personal Pension Plan, or used to buy back into the national social security system if the distribution is from contracted-out contributions.

Funds can also be used to purchase an insurance policy or annuity contract. Any member of a pension plan—not just job leavers—may ask for a transfer value or cash equivalent of his/her accrued pension rights. The plan trustees must arrange for the transfer to a statutory alternative chosen by the member. Although it may occur anytime, this transfer usually occurs at job change.

The United Kingdom provides two options for portable individual retirement savings. First, workers enrolled in private pension plans are entitled to purchase Free-Standing Additional Voluntary Contributions from an insurance company, provided the combined benefits to which they are entitled do not exceed statutory limits for tax exemption. These contributions allow members of employer-sponsored plans to increase retirement benefits through individual contributions, similar to an IRA. Such benefits are portable because, like individual account plans, they are not tied to an employer. The second option extends Personal Pension Plan eligibility to all employed individuals regardless of whether they participate in an employer-sponsored plan. Workers covered by a private pension may opt out of that arrangement and set up a Personal Pension Plan. Instead of preserving a job-leaver's benefit rights within the plan, a British worker may use the accrued rights to purchase an annuity. A plan used for contracting-out may pay a premium to government to repurchase in social security pension rights that would have replaced social security benefits.

Some British plans reject asset transfers or only accept transfers for workers below a set age. This occurs when the employer would be forced to subsidize prior service in a salary-related plan. Some plans guarantee to index pension rights in line with earnings. If the member suffers a pay cut in a new job, he/she may opt to retain rights in a prior plan.

The United Kingdom offers job leavers many pension options because British Conservative political philosophy highly values individual choice. With the range of options, however, individuals may "game the system," seeking the arrangement most favorable to their circumstances. The more options available, the more serious is this problem of adverse selection, with workers of like attributes bunching into the pension types most favorable to their life expectancy or income. Current U.K. pension law has been fully in place for only a few years, and more time is needed to evaluate whether so many choices will create funding problems for any plans due to adverse selection in plan choice.

CONCLUSIONS

The Netherlands, the United Kingdom, and Canada have done more than the United States to cut portability losses. These countries require short vesting periods and stringently restrict lump sum distributions. The Netherlands and the United Kingdom index vested benefits for most early leavers.

Japan and the United States are the only countries in this group allowing virtually unrestricted lump sum distributions at job change. In the other countries, retirement benefits are preserved by requiring workers to use one or more options: retain benefits with the prior employer, transfer vested benefits to the new employer, or transfer benefits to a portability vehicle like an IRA, where the benefits lock in until retirement.

What lessons can be learned from countries with more pension portability than the United States? Many American and Canadian observers suggest that the cost of indexing benefits for early leavers (people with deferred vested benefits) would greatly reduce pension plan growth. Though it has not been rigorously analyzed, the experience in the Netherlands and the United Kingdom appears to reject that position.

NOTES

1. This chapter draws heavily on material presented in Turner and Dailey (1991), and especially Andrews (1991). For further information about private pension systems in other countries, refer to Turner and Dailey (1991).

2. For example, this chapter does not discuss the issues of pension portability across national borders, which European pension policy analysts are currently discussing because of the creation of a single European labor market (see Jolliffe 1990).

3. This chapter compares the countries feature by feature. For an explanation of portability on a country-by-country basis, see Turner and Dailey (1991).

4. For a discussion of portability in Japan, see Murakami (1991).

5. Vesting is not required in Greece, Ireland, Italy, Luxembourg, Portugal and Belgium (for self-administered plans) (Jolliffe 1990).

6. In the United Kingdom, the statutory requirement to revalue vested benefit rights originally existed only for benefit rights accruing since January 1, 1985. Under the Social Security Act of 1990, the requirement now applies to all accrued benefits.

7. An additional technical calculation must then be made to determine the number of years of service credited under the new plan. For example, assume that two plans have identical benefit structures, except that the gaining plan provides a benefit at age 60 of 1.5 percent of final pay for each year of service while the losing plan only provides a benefit at age 65 of 1.25 percent of final pay. The 40-year-old member with 10 years of service was making $40,000 a year at termination with the first employer and started with the second employer at $45,000 a year. The 10 years of service would be shortened (to 4.82 years) for purposes of calculating benefits in the new plan because the new benefit accrual rate and salary base are both greater. Both the old and the new employers are responsible for funding any actuarial loss generated in their own plans by the portability transfer.

8. For a discussion of portability in Canada see Conklin (1991).

9. This discussion of portability in the United Kingdom is drawn largely from Birmingham (1991).

13

Conclusions
Tradeoffs and Options

Any changes in portability policy will be made after balancing competing interests. Policies that help one group or further some of their goals may hurt another group or detract from their goals. Direct and indirect costs diminish the extent goals are achieved or interest groups are helped. Workers and firms may undo mandated changes in income flows by changing compensation outside the pension plan.

Before making decisions, policymakers must clarify priorities among goals and between groups. This book provides no answers about priorities, which are ultimately political decisions, but clarifies many of the conflicts and tradeoffs. This final chapter summarizes conflicting interests that should be considered in making portability policy and offers a selective list of policies that will reduce portability losses.

For several reasons, portability policies that rely on a job leaver finding another job with a pension will not work well in the United States. Econometric evidence indicates that although firms offering pensions employ older workers, they are less likely to hire older workers. This finding is supported by statistics showing that many workers, especially women, who had a pension on a previous job did not have one on their current job.

Econometric studies suggest that making pensions portable will have only a small effect on job mobility in the United States. Pensions alone do not inhibit mobility much. Pension-covered workers are less likely to change jobs than noncovered workers for a number of reasons: (1) people covered by pensions are less likely to be laid off; (2) jobs offering pensions tend to select workers who are less likely to change jobs; (3) jobs offering pensions tend to pay a high enough wage to discourage job change; and (4) other aspects of compensation, such as retiree health benefits, also discourage job change.

TRADEOFFS AMONG WORKERS

Many portability options raise benefits for short-tenure workers. The net increase in wealth for these workers and the presumed decrease in wealth for long-tenure workers depends, however, on whether workers pay for pension reform with reduced wages. If that is the case, then gains or losses in wealth due to pension reform will be offset by changes in wages. The wage-pension tradeoff, however, probably results in an imperfect adjustment of compensation costs because it is not possible to perfectly determine in advance who will be a short-tenure worker.

The interests of women, who traditionally have had more job mobility than men, may be favored by portability policy. But mobility statistics comparing full-time male and female workers overstate the difference because women covered by a pension have job mobility that more closely resembles job mobility of men. Portability policy will raise labor market efficiency for some workers by lowering the cost of changing jobs, but may reduce labor market efficiency for others by discouraging long tenure and investment in job skills. The balance between these two groups will vary depending upon factors such as import competition and technological changes that affect the stability of employment in the economy.

TRADEOFFS BETWEEN WORKERS AND EMPLOYERS

If portability policy reduces employer willingness to offer a pension plan or causes employers to offer defined contribution plans when workers would rather have defined benefit plans, employees may be hurt. Because portability policy would reduce income gains from job stability, firms would use defined benefit pension plans less frequently for retaining and rewarding long-service workers. Firms needing highly trained and stable workforces may be hurt relative to firms where high labor turnover has little effect on the firm's costs.

TRADEOFFS BETWEEN GOALS

In government budgeting, portability policies that cost the treasury tax revenue must compete with other possible cash expenditures and tax expenditures of government funds. More fundamentally, the goals of labor market efficiency, retirement income adequacy, greater national savings, governmental nonintervention, and tax equity may conflict. Pension portability may raise retirement income while reducing efficiency for some firms where long worker tenure is needed because of the lengthy worker training required. The goal of greater national savings could possibly be achieved via unrestricted IRAs. That goal, however, may conflict with tax equity if the tax benefits go largely to high income workers.

With the possible negative and positive effects of portability policy, along with little evidence on the relative importance of various tradeoffs, it could be argued by a self-interested party that any major policy would be "the straw that broke the back of defined benefit plans." In this regard, foreign experience provides a good idea of the range of feasible policies and suggests that the United States could do a lot more to reduce the pension benefit losses of job changers.

The United Kingdom, the Netherlands, and, to a lesser extent, Canada have all gone further than the United States in reducing the portability losses suffered by a mobile workforce. All three countries have virtually ended preretirement lump sum distributions. The United Kingdom and the Netherlands have indexed benefits for deferred vested (early) job leavers. Of less importance, all three offer more rapid vesting than the United States. Japan, however, reflecting the view of the productivity- raising effect of a lifetime commitment to one job, has done much less than the United States to reduce pension benefit loss due to job change.

Policy Options

A wide range of feasible options could reduce the loss of pension benefits due to job change. The following is a selective list.

1. Prohibit plans that grant lower percentage cost-of-living adjustments for retirees with less service or who end employment prior to retirement.

2. Prohibit plans from requiring a later age for initial benefit receipt for workers ending employment prior to retirement.

3. In defined contribution plans, prohibit contribution rates that rise with service, age, or earnings.

4. In defined contribution plans, prohibit the distribution of forfeited account balances to remaining participants based on account balances. Instead, require that the distribution be based on annual contributions or earnings.

5. In defined benefit plans, prohibit plans from having formulas with higher accrual rates at higher years worked or older ages.

6. Reduce to four the years required for vesting for both multiemployer and single-employer plans.

7. Require that preretirement lump sum distributions from defined benefit plans be calculated using a real interest rate, such as 3 percent.

8. Prohibit preretirement lump sum distributions except at job change for small sums or for financial hardship. Alternatively, require that all sums withdrawn from a pension before retirement be rolled over into an IRA. These restrictions could be limited to workers age 30 to 59.

9. Require inflation indexing up to 4 percent annually of wages used to figure benefits for early leavers in final-pay plans. Alternatively, require such indexing only for early leavers who have worked 10 or more years for the employer.

10. Require flat-benefit plans and career-average plans to upgrade benefits for early leavers using the same formula that they use for current workers.

11. Require firms to provide extra years of credit in defined benefit plans and extra contributions in defined contribution plans for laid-off workers.

12. Amend the Trade Adjustment Assistance Act so that displaced workers are compensated for lost pension benefits as well as lost wages.

American workers using the political system have increasingly required firms to provide pension benefits that are unreduced by job change. That trend is likely to continue. This book has shown that many policy options could be chosen to further protect pension benefits from losses that occur when workers change jobs.

REFERENCES

Allen, Steven G., Robert Clark, and Ann McDermed. 1986. "Job Mobility, Older Workers and the Role of Pensions." Report to the U.S. Department of Labor, Contract No. J-9-M-5-0049, October.

_____. 1988. "The Pension Cost of Changing Jobs," *Research on Aging* 10: 459-471.

_____. 1990. "Pensions, Bonding, and Lifetime Jobs." Mimeograph, North Carolina State University.

_____. 1992. "Post-retirement Benefit Increases in the 1980s." In *Trends in Pensions 1992,* John A. Turner and Daniel J. Beller, eds. Washington, DC: Government Printing Office.

Andrews, Emily S. 1985. *The Changing Profile of Pensions in America.* Washington, DC: Employee Benefit Research Institute.

_____. 1989. *Pension Policy and Small Employers: At What Price Coverage?* Washington DC: Employee Benefit Research Institute.

_____. 1990a. "The Potential Labor Market Effects of Legislative Proposals to Enhance Pension Portability: A Review of the Literature." Report for the U.S. Department of Labor, Pension and Welfare Benefits Administration, February.

_____. 1990b. "Retirement Savings and Lump Sum Distributions." Prepared for the U.S. Department of Labor, Pension and Welfare Benefits Administration, May 1990.

_____. 1991. "Pension Portability in Five Countries." In *Pension Policy: An International Perspective,* John A. Turner and Lorna M. Dailey, eds. Washington, DC: Government Printing Office.

Andrews, Emily S., and Michael D. Hurd. 1992. "Employee Benefits and Retirement Income Adequacy: Data, Research and Policy Issues." In *Pensions and the Economy,* Zvi Bodie and Alicia Munnell, eds. Philadelphia: Pension Research Council.

Atkins, F. Roger. 1991. "Some Observations on International Developments." Presented at an Employee Benefit Research Institute—Education and Research Fund policy forum, May 2.

Atkins, Lawrence F. 1986. *Spend It or Save It? Pension Lump-Sum Distributions and Tax Reform.* Washington, DC: Employee Benefit Research Institute, Washington, DC.

Ball, David George. 1990. "Testimony of David George Ball, Assistant Secretary for Pension and Welfare Benefits Administration, U.S. Department of Labor before the Subcommittee on Private Retirement Plans and Oversight of the Internal Revenue Service of the Senate Committee on Finance," August 3.

Barron, John M., Dan A. Black, and Mark A. Loewenstein. 1987. "Employer Size: Wage Growth," *Journal of Labor Economics* 5 (January): 76-89.

Becker, Gary. 1964. *Human Capital: A Theoretical and Empirical Analysis.* New York: Columbia University Press.

Becker, Gary, and George Stigler. 1974. "Law Enforcement, Malfeasance and Compensation of Officers," *Journal of Legal Studies* 3: 1-18.

Beller, Daniel J. 1989. "Coverage and Vesting Patterns in Private Pension Plans, 1975-1985." In *Trends in Pensions,* John A. Turner and Daniel J. Beller, eds. Washington, DC: Government Printing Office.

Beller, Daniel J., and Helen H. Lawrence. 1992. "Trends in Private Pension Plan Coverage." In *Trends in Pensions 1992,* John A. Turner and Daniel J. Beller, eds. Washington, DC: Government Printing Office.

Beller, Daniel J., and David D. McCarthy. 1992. "Private Pension Benefit Amounts." In *Trends in Pensions 1992,* John A. Turner and Daniel J. Beller, eds. Washington, DC: Government Printing Office.

Bergmann, Barbara R. 1986. *The Economic Emergence of Women.* New York: Basic Books.

Berry, Steve, Peter Gottschalk, and Doug Wissoker. 1988. "An Error Components Model of the Impact of Plant Closings on Earnings," *Review of Economics and Statistics* 70 (November): 701-707.

Birmingham, William. 1991. "Occupational and Personal Pension Provision in the United Kingdom." In *Pension Policy: An International Perspective,* edited by John A. Turner and Lorna M. Dailey. Washington, DC: Government Printing Office.

Blau, Francine D., and Lawrence M. Kahn. 1981. "Causes and Consequences of Layoffs," *Economic Inquiry* 19 (April): 270- 296.

Bodie, Zvi, and Leslie E. Papke. 1990. "Pension Portfolio and Investment Strategies." Final Report to the U.S. Department of Labor, Contract No. J-9-P-8-0097, May.

Browne, Lynn E. 1985. "Structural Change and Dislocated Workers," *New England Economic Review* (January/February): 15-30.

Brownlee, H. J. 1989. "Pension Portability: Would It Really Work?" *Contingencies* (May/June): 50-55.

Bulow, Jeremy. 1982. "What are Corporate Pension Liabilities?" *Quarterly Journal of Economics* 97: 435-452.

Bureau of National Affairs. Daily Executive Report, July 13, 1988.

_____. *Daily Labor Report.* August 9, 1990.

Chernoff, Joel. 1990. "IRS Eases Benefit Disbursement Rulees," *Pensions and Investments* (October): 18.

Choate, Pat, and J. K. Linger. 1986. *The Hi-Flex Society.* New York: Alfred A. Knop.

Christl, Donald J. 1991. "Age Weighteu Profit Sharing Plans Offer New Design Opportunities," *WEB Network* (May).

Conklin, David W. 1991. "Pension Policy Reforms in Canada." In *Pension Policy: An International Perspective,* John A. Turner and Lorna M. Dailey, eds. Washington, DC: Government Printing Office.

Cornwell, Christopher, and Stuart Dorsey. 1989. "Temporary Layoffs and Pensions." Mimeograph, University of Georgia.

Cornwell, Christopher, Stuart Dorsey, and Nasser Mehrzad. 1991. "Opportunistic Behavior by Firms in Implicit Pension Contracts," *Journal of Human Resources* 26: 704-725.

Curme, Michael, and Lawrence M. Kahn. 1990. "The Impact of the Threat of Bankruptcy on the Structure of Compensation," *Journal of Labor Economics* 8 (4).

Davis, S. J., and J. Haltiwanger. 1989. "Gross Job Creation, Gross Job Destruction and Employment Reallocation." Unpublished paper.

Daykin, Christopher D. 1991. "Pension Policy Statistics in the United Kingdom." In *Pension Policy: An International Perspective.* John A. Turner and Lorna M. Dailey, eds. Washington, DC: Government Printing Office.

Devens, Richard M. 1986. "Displaced Workers: One Year Later," *Monthly Labor Review* 109 (July): 40-43.

Doescher, Tabitha A. 1991. "The Effect of Portability on Pension Benefit Losses Associated with Involuntary Layoffs." Report to the U.S. Department of Labor, Pension and Welfare Benefits Administration, January.

Doescher, Tabitha A., and Stuart Dorsey. 1992. "Pension Benefit Losses of Job Losers and Offsetting Compensation." Unpublished paper.

Doescher, Tabitha A., and John A. Turner. 1988. "Social Security Benefits and the Baby Boom Generation," *American Economic Review* 78 (May): 76-80.

Dopkeen, J. 1987. "Postretirement Health Benefits," *Health Services Research Report* 21 (February).

Dorsey, Stuart. 1987. "The Economic Function of Private Pensions: An Empirical Analysis," *Journal of Labor Economics* 5, part 2 (October): S171-S189.

_____. 1990. "Pension Portability and Labor Market Efficiency." Report submitted to the U.S. Department of Labor, Pension and Welfare Benefits Administration, September.

Dunne, Timothy, Mark J. Roberts, and Larry Samuelson. 1989. "The Growth and Failure of U.S. Manufacturing Plants," *Quarterly Journal of Economics* 104 (November): 671-698.

Economic Report of the President. 1990. Washington, DC: Government Printing Office.

Employee Benefit Research Institute. 1986a. "Pension Vesting Standards: ERISA and Beyond," *EBRI Issue Brief* 51 (February).

_____. 1986b. "Pension Portability and Benefit Adequacy," EBRI Issue Brief 56 (July).

_____. 1990. *Fundamentals of Employee Benefit Programs,* 4th edition. Washington, DC: EBRI.

Employment and Training Report of the President, 1982.

Even, William E., and David A. Macpherson. 1990a. "Employer Size and Compensation: The Case of Pensions." Miami University, Oxford, Ohio, August.

_____. 1990b. "Plant Size and the Decline of Unionism," *Economic Letters* 32: 393-398.

Farber, Henry S. "The Recent Decline in Unionization in the United States," *Science* 238: 915-920.

Flaim, Paul O., and Ellen Sehgal. 1985. "Displaced Workers of 1979- 83: How Well Have They Fared?" *Monthly Labor Review* 8 (June): 3-16.

Foley, Jill. 1990. "International Benefits: Part Two—Retirement Benefits," *EBRI Issue Brief* 107 (October).

Fu Associates. 1990. *Lump Sum Distributions: A Comparison of Administrative and Survey Data.* Arlington, VA: Fu Associates, 1990.

Fuchs, Victor R. 1989. Women's Quest for Economic Equality," *Journal of Economic Perspectives* 3 (Winter): 25-41.

Garen, John E. 1985. "Worker Heterogeneity, Job Screening, and Firm Size," *Journal of Political Economy* 93 (August): 715-739.

Graham, Avy D. 1988. "How Has Vesting Changed Since Passage of Employee Retirement Income Security Act?" *Monthly Labor Review* 11 (August): 20-25.

Grubbs, Donald S., Jr. 1981. "Study and Analysis of Portability and Reciprocity in Single-Employer Pension Funds." Final report prepared under contract to U.S. Department of Labor, July.

Gustman, Alan L., and Olivia S. Mitchell. 1991. "Pensions and Labor Market Activity: Behavior and Data Requirements." In *Pensions and the Economy,* Zvi Bodie and Alicia Munnell, eds. Philadelphia: Pension Research Council.

Gustman, Alan L., and Thomas L. Steinmeier. 1987. "Pensions, Efficiency Wages, and Job Mobility." Working Paper No. 2426. National Bureau of Economic Research, November.

_____. 1989a. "An Analysis of Pension Benefit Formulas, Pension Wealth and Incentives from Pensions." In *Research In Labor Economics* 10, Ronald Ehrenberg, ed. Greenwich, CT: JAI Press.

_____. 1989b. "Evaluating Pension Policies in a Model with Endogenous Contributions." NBER Working Paper 3085. August.

_____. 1990. "Pension Portability and Labor Mobility: Evidence from the Survey of Income and Program Participation." Report to the U.S. Department of Labor, Pension and Welfare Benefits Administration, July.

Haber, Sheldon E., Enrique J. Lamas, and Gordon Green. 1983. "A New Method for Estimating Job Separations by Sex and Race," *Monthly Labor Review* 106 (June): 20-27.

Hall, Robert E. 1982. "The Importance of Lifetime Jobs in the U.S. Economy," *American Economic Review* 72: 716-724.

Hamermesh, Daniel S. 1989. "What Do We Know About Worker Displacement in the U.S?" *Industrial Relations* 28 (Winter): 51-59.

Hay/Huggins Company, Inc. 1988. "The Effect of Job Mobility on Pension Benefits." Report to the U. S. Department of Labor, Contract No. J-9-P-7-0044, July.

_____. 1990a. "The Transfer of Benefits and Assets in Portable Defined Benefit Plans." Produced for the U.S. Department of Labor, June.

_____. 1990b. "Projection of Mix of DB/DC Plans to the Year 2000." Produced for the U.S. Department of Labor, December.

_____. 1991. "Projection of Total Portability Loss." Produced for the U.S. Department of Labor, February.

Herz, Diane E. 1990. "Worker Displacement in a Period of Rapid Job Expansion: 1983-87," *Monthly Labor Review* 113 (May): 21-33.

Hewitt Associates. 1980. *Survey Results: Lump Sum Distribution Options in Pension Plans Covering Salaried Employees.* Lincolnshire, IL: Hewitt Associates.

_____. 1989. *Lump Sum Options and Postretirement Increases in Pension Plans, 1989.* Lincolnshire, IL: Hewitt Associates.

Horvath, Francis W. 1983. "Estimates of Eventual Job Tenure for the U.S. Labor Force, 1981." Proceedings of the Social Statistics Section, Annual Meeting of the American Statistical Association, Toronto, Canada.

_____. 1987. "The Pulse of Economic Change: Displaced Workers of 1981-85," *Monthly Labor Review* 110 (June): 3-12.

Howland, Marie, and George E. Peterson. 1988. "Labor Market Conditions and the Reemployment of Displaced Workers," *Industrial and Labor Relations Review* 42 (October): 109-122.

Hutchens, Robert. 1986. "Delayed Payment Contracts and a Firm's Propensity to Hire Older Workers," *Journal of Labor Economics* 3 (October): 439-452.

_____. 1987. "A Test of Lazear's Theory of Delayed Payment Contracts," *Journal of Labor Economics* 4 (October): S153- S170.

Ippolito, Richard A. 1985. "The Labor Contract and True Economic Pension Liabilities," *American Economic Review* 75 (December): 1031-43.

_____. 1986a. "The Economics of Pensions and Mobility." Report to the U.S. Department of Labor.

_____. 1986b. *Pensions, Economics and Public Policy.* Homewood, IL: Dow Jones-Irwin.

Joint Committee on Taxation. 1988. "Proposals and Issues Relating to the Portability of Pension Plan Benefits." Washington, DC: Government Printing Office, July 11.

Jolliffe, J. A. 1990. "The Portability of Occupational Pensions within Europe." Prepared for the International Seminar on the Future of Basic and Supplementary Pension Schemes in the European Community—1992 and Beyond. Watsons Europe, Surrey, January.

Jovanovic, Boyan. 1979. "Firm-Specific Capital and Turnover," *Journal of Political Economy* 87: 1246-1260.

Jovanovic, Boyan, and Jacob Mincer. 1978. "Labor Mobility and Wages." Unpublished paper, Columbia University, June.

Jovanovic, Boyan, and Robert Moffit. 1990. "An Estimate of a Sectoral Model of Labor Mobility." NBER Working Paper No. 3227.

Katz, Lawrence F., and Lawrence H. Summers. 1989. "Industry Rents: Evidence and Implications." *Brookings Papers on Economic Activity.*

Keizer, Piet J. C. 1991. "Pension Policy Statistics in the Netherlands." In *Pension Policy: An International Perspective,* John A. Turner and Lorna M. Dailey, eds. Washington, DC: Government Printing Office.

Klerman, Jacob, Joan L. Buchanan, and Arleen Leibowitz. 1990. "Labor Turnover and Health Insurance." RAND Corporation, May.

Kolodrubetz, Walter W., and Donald M. Landay. 1973. "Coverage and Vesting of Full-Time Employees Under Private Retirement Plans," *Social Security Bulletin* 36 (November): 20-36.

Korczyk, Sophie M. 1990. "Pension Portability Issues Affecting Women." U.S. Department of Labor, Pension and Welfare Benefits Administration, June.

_____. 1992. "Gender and Pension Coverage." In *Trends in Pensions 1992,* John A. Turner and Daniel J. Beller, eds. Washington, DC: Government Printing Office.

Kotlikoff, Laurence J., and Daniel E. Smith. 1983. *Pensions in the American Economy.* Chicago: University of Chicago Press.

Kotlikoff, Laurence J., and David A. Wise. 1985. "Labor Compensation and the Structure of Private Pension Plans: Evidence for Contractual vs. Spot Labor Markets." In *Pensions, Labor, and Individual Choices*, David A. Wise, ed. Chicago: University of Chicago Press.

_____. 1987. "The Incentive Effects of Private Pension Plans." In *Issues in Pension Economics*, Z. Bodie, J. Shoven, and D. Wise, eds. Chicago: University of Chicago Press.

_____. 1989. *The Wage Carrot and the Pension Stick.* Kalamazoo, MI: W.E. Upjohn Institute.

Kruse, Douglas. 1989. "Profit Sharing and Employment Variability: Microeconomic Evidence on the Weitzman Theory." Rutgers University, May.

Lawrence, Helen H. 1989. "Trends in Private Pension Plans." In *Trends in Pensions,* John A. Turner and Daniel J. Beller, eds. Washington, DC: Government Printing Office.

Lazear, Edward P. 1979. "Why is There Mandatory Retirement?" *Journal of Political Economy* 87 (December): 1261-1284.

Leonard, Johnathan S. 1987. "In the Wrong Place at the Wrong Time: The Extent of Frictional and Structural Unemployment." In *Unemployment and the Structure of Labor Markets,* K. Lang and J. Leonard, eds. Oxford: Basil Blackwell, 1987.

Leonard, Johnathan S. and Louis Jacobson. 1990. "Earnings Inequality and Job Turnover," *American Economic Review* 80 (May): 298-302.

Lockhart, James B. 1990. "The Future of Defined Benefit Pension Plans," *Employee Benefits Digest* 27 (November): 3-5.

Madden, Janice Fanning. 1988. "The Distribution of Economic Losses among Displaced Workers: Measurement Methods Matter," *Journal of Human Resources* 23 (Winter): 93-107.

Maxwell, Nan L. 1989. "Labor Market Effects from Involuntary Job Losses in Layoffs, Plant Closings: The Role of Human Capital in Facilitating Reemployment and Reduced Wage Losses, *American Journal of Economics and Sociology* 48 (April): 129-141.

Maxwell, Nan L., and Ronald J. D'Amico. 1986. "Employment and Wage Effects of Involuntary Job Separation: Male-Female Differences," *American Economic Review* 76 (May 1986): 373- 377.

McCarthy, David. 1985. "Findings From the Survey of Private Pension Benefit Amounts." U.S. Department of Labor, Office of Pension and Welfare Benefit Programs.

McDonald, M. E. 1975. *Reciprocity Among Private Multiemployer Pension Plans.* Homewood, IL: Richard D. Irwin.

McGill, Dan M. 1972. *Preservation of Pension Benefit Rights*. Published for the Pension Research Council, Wharton School of Finance and Commerce, University of Pennsylvania by Richard D. Irwin, Homewood, IL.

Meier, Elizabeth L., and Preston C. Bassett. 1981. "Technical Papers," Chapter 16 in the report of the President's Commission on Pension Policy. Washington, DC: Government Printing Office.

Mincer, Jacob. 1988. "Job Training, Wage Growth, and Labor Turnover." NBER Working Paper No. 2690, 1988.

_____. 1989. "Human Capital Responses to Technological Change in the Labor Market." Working Paper No. 3207, National Bureau of Economic Research.

Mincer, Jacob and Haim Ofek. 1982. "Interrupted Work Careers: Depreciation and Restoration of Human Capital," *Journal of Human Resources* 17 (Winter): 3-24.

Mitchell, Daniel J. B. 1989. "Wage Pressures and Labor Shortages: The 1960s and 1980s," *Brookings Papers on Economic Activity* 2: 191-231.

Mitchell, Olivia S. 1982. "Fringe Benefits and Labor Mobility," *Journal of Human Resources* 17 (Spring): 286-298.

_____. 1983. "Fringe Benefits and the Cost of Changing Jobs," *Industrial and Labor Relations Review* 37 (October): 70-78.

_____. 1986. "Encouraging Later Retirement: Where and How is it Working." Final Report to the Social Security Administration, January.

_____. 1991. "The Effects of Mandating Benefits Packages," *Research in Labor Economics*.

_____. 1992. "Pension Plan Retirement Formulas and Benefit Provisions: Evidence from BLS Employee Benefits Survey Data." In *Trends in Pensions 1992*, John A. Turner and Daniel J. Beller, eds. Washington, DC: Government Printing Office.

Murakami, Kiyoshi. 1991. "Severance and Retirement Benefits in Japan." In *Pension Policy: An International Perspective*, John A. Turner and Lorna M. Dailey, eds. Washington, DC: Government Printing Office.

Murphy, Kevin and Robert Toppel. 1987. "The Evaluation of Unemployment in the United States: 1968-85." In *NBER Macroeconomic Annual 1987*, Stanley Fischer, ed. Cambridge, MA: MIT Press.

Oi, Walter Y. 1962. "Labor as a Quasi-Fixed Factor," *Journal of Political Economy* 70 (December): 538-555.

_____. 1983. "Heterogeneous Firms and the Organization of Production," *Economic Inquiry* 21 (April): 147-71.

Ozanne, Larry, and David Lindeman. 1987. "Tax Policy for Pensions and other Retirement Saving." Congressional Budget Office, April.

Parnes, Herbert S., Mary G. Gagen, and Randall H. King. 1981. "Job Loss Among Long-Service Workers." In *Work and Retirement: A Longitudinal Study of Men*, Herbert S. Parnes et al., eds. Cambridge: MIT Press.

Parnes, Herbert S., and Randy King. 1977. "Middle-aged Job Losers," *Industrial Gerontology* (Spring): 77-95.

Pensions and Investments. August 20, 1990.

Pension Rights Center. 1990-1991. *News from the Pension Rights Center* (Winter).

Piacentini, Joseph. 1989. "Pension Coverage and Benefit Entitlement: New Findings for 1988," *EBRI Issue Brief* 94 (September).

_____. 1990a. "Preservation of Pension Benefits." *EBRI Issue Brief* 98 (January).

_____. 1990b. "An Analysis of Pension Participation at Current and Prior Jobs, Receipt and Use of Lump-Sum Distributions, and Tenure at Current Job." Report to the U.S. Department of Labor, Pension and Welfare Benefits Administration, April.

Plunkert, Lois M. 1990. "The 1980s: A Decade of Job Growth and Industry Shifts," *Monthly Labor Review* 113 (September): 3- 16.

Podgursky, Michael, and Paul Swaim. 1987. "Job Displacement and Earnings Loss: Evidence from the Displaced Worker Survey," *Industrial and Labor Relations Review* 41 (October): 17-29.

Profit Sharing Research Foundation. 1989. "Profit Sharing Plan Loans: Availability, Use and Amounts." *Report* 1989-4, Profit Sharing Research Foundation.

Quinn, Joseph F., Richard V. Burkhauser, and Daniel A. Myers. 1990. *Passing the Torch: The Influence of Economic Incentives on Work and Retirement*. Kalamazoo, MI: W.E. Upjohn Institute.

Ross, Arthur. 1958. "Do We Have a New Industrial Feudalism?" *American Economic Review* 48 (December): 1144-1175.

Ruhm, Christopher J. 1987. "The Economic Consequences of Labor Mobility," *Industrial and Labor Relations Review* 41 (October): 30-42.

Sahin, Izzet. 1989. *Private Pensions and Employee Mobility*. New York: Quorum Books.

Salop, Joanne, and Steven Salop. 1976. "Self Selection and Turnover in the Labor Market," *Quarterly Journal of Economics* 90: 619-627.

Schieber, Sylvester. 1990. *Benefits Bargain: Why We Should Not Tax Employee Benefits*. Washington, DC: Association of Private Pension and Welfare Plans.

Schiller, Bradley, and Randall D. Weiss. 1979. "The Impact of Private Pensions on Firm Attachment," *Review of Economics and Statistics* (August): 369-380.

Schmitt, Ray. 1988. "Pension Portability: What Does it Mean? How Does it Work? What Does it Accomplish?" Congressional Research Service, June 28.

Sehgal, Ellen. 1984. "Occupational Mobility and Job Tenure in 1983," *Monthly Labor Review* 107: 18-23.

Seitchik, Adam, and Jeffrey Zornitsky. 1989. *From One Job to the Next: Worker Adjustment in a Changing Labor Market.* Kalamazoo, MI: W.E. Upjohn Institute.

Sing, Bill. 1990. "A Changing Outlook for Retiree Health Plans," *Los Angeles Times,* October 28.

Turner, John A., and Daniel J. Beller (eds.). 1989. *Trends in Pensions.* Washington, DC: Government Printing Office.

_____ (eds.). 1992. *Trends in Pensions 1992.* Washington, DC: Government Printing Office.

Turner, John A., Daniel J. Beller, and William J. Wiatrowski (eds.). 1993. *Trends in Health Benefits.* Washington, DC: Government Printing Office.

Turner, John A., and Lorna M. Dailey (eds.). 1991. *Pension Policy: An International Perspective.* Washington, DC: Government Printing Office.

U.S. Department of Labor, Bureau of Labor Statistics. 1985. "Displaced Workers: 1979-83." Bulletin 2240. July.

_____. 1990. *Employee Benefits in Medium and Large Firms, 1989.* Washington, DC: Government Printing Office, June.

U.S. General Accounting Office. 1986. "Displaced Workers: Extent of Business Closures, Layoffs, and the Public and Private Response." GAO/HRD-86-116BR, July.

_____. 1988. "401(k) Plans: Incidence, Provisions, and Benefits." GAO/PEND-88-15BR.

_____. 1990 "Private Pensions: Impact of New Vesting Rules Similar for Women and Men." GAO/HRD-90-101, August.

Warshawsky, Mark. 1992. *The Uncertain Promise of Retiree Health Benefits.* Washington, DC: American Enterprise Institute Press.

Weiss, Andrew, and Henry J. Landau. 1984. "Wages, Hiring Standards, and Firm Size," *Journal of Labor Economics* 2 (October): 477- 99.

Wiatrowski, William J. 1993. "The Incidence of Employee Benefits." In *Trends in Health Benefits,* John A. Turner, Daniel J. Beller, and William J. Wiatrowski, eds. Washington, DC: Government Printing Office.

Wolf, Douglas A., and Frank Levy. 1984. "Pension Coverage, Pension Vesting and the Distribution of Job Tenure." In *Retirement and Economic Behavior,* Henry J. Aaron and Gary Burtless, eds. Washington, DC: Brookings Institution.

Woods, John R. 1989. "Pension Coverage Among Private Wage and Salary Workers: Preliminary Findings from the 1988 Survey of Employee Benefits, *Social Security Bulletin* 52 (October): 2- 19.

Wyatt Company. 1990. *The Compensation and Benefits File* 6 (September).

Yumiba, Yoshihiro. 1991. "Pension Policy Statistics in Japan." In *Pension Policy: An International Perspective,* John A. Turner and Lorna M. Dailey, eds. Washington, DC: Government Printing Office.

Zedlewski, Sheila Rafferty. 1986. "A Model of Pension Preferences of Married Women." Report to the U.S. Department of Health and Human Services under Grant No. 84-ASPE135A, March 18.

INDEX

About the Institute

The W.E. Upjohn Institute for Employment Research is a nonprofit research organization devoted to finding and promoting solutions to employment-related problems at the national, state, and local level. It is an activity of the W.E. Upjohn Unemployment Trustee Corporation, which was established in 1932 to administer a fund set aside by the late Dr. W.E. Upjohn, founder of The Upjohn Company, to seek ways to counteract the loss of employment income during economic downturns.

The Institute is funded largely by income from the W.E. Upjohn Unemployment Trust, supplemented by outside grants, contracts, and sales of publications. Activities of the Institute are comprised of the following elements: (1) a research program conducted by a resident staff of professional social scientists; (2) a competitive grant program, which expands and complements the internal research program by providing financial support to researchers outside the Institute; (3) a publications program, which provides the major vehicle for the dissemination of research by staff and grantees, as well as other selected work in the field; and (4) an Employment Management Services division, which manages most of the publicly funded employment and training programs in the local area.

The broad objectives of the Institute's research, grant, and publication programs are to: (1) promote scholarship and experimentation on issues of public and private employment and unemployment policy; and (2) make knowledge and scholarship relevant and useful to policymakers in their pursuit of solutions to employment and unemployment problems.

Current areas of concentration for these programs include: causes, consequences, and measures to alleviate unemployment; social insurance and income maintenance programs; compensation; workforce quality; work arrangements; family labor issues; labor-management relations; and regional economic development and local labor markets.